Pocket Guide to
Sheds

D1612432

013750144 9

Pocket Guide to
Sheds

Gordon Thorburn

First published in Great Britain in 2011 by
Remember When
An imprint of
Pen & Sword Books Ltd
47 Church Street
Barnsley
South Yorkshire
S70 2AS

ISBN 978 1 84468 127 3

A CIP catalogue record for this book is
available from the British Library.

Typeset in 10pt Minion by Mac Style, Beverley, East Yorkshire
Printed and bound in the UK by CPI

Cover photograph by John Manning

Pen & Sword Books Ltd incorporates the imprints of Pen & Sword Aviation,
Pen & Sword Maritime, Pen & Sword Military, Wharncliffe Local History,
Pen & Sword Select, Pen & Sword Military Classics, Leo Cooper, Seaforth
Publishing and Frontline Publishing.

For a complete list of Pen & Sword titles please contact
PEN & SWORD BOOKS LIMITED
47 Church Street, Barnsley, South Yorkshire, S70 2AS, England
E-mail: enquiries@pen-and-sword.co.uk
Website: www.pen-and-sword.co.uk

Contents

Introduction

Enter the Golden Age

As the globe warms, everything runs out and people become the willing slaves of small electronic machines, we have our response: the Golden Age of Sheds.

We can look out from our sheds and see those unfortunates, the slaves in question, the ones who would rather be stripped naked and whipped through the market square than be separated, for one nanosecond, from their portable telephones and i-thingies, and we can smile.

This book is where the smilers are. Here, you can find the man who reinvigorates the *entente cordiale* in wood, the woman who boils kettles, the woman who says 'I'm Nicola from In the Shed', the man who says 'What's

yours?' the dooket that Jock built, the blockhouse that Noah built, a neoclassical stately home, and all manner of things musical, yogic, animalcular, roguish, ockerish and cloudy.

Whether we see our shed as a place of work, a place of fun, a welcome refuge from normality, a shaded pool of tranquility, a realisation of a secret yearning, a place to pot up the geraniums, or a little bit of all of those, we Sheddies, tribesfolk of the mighty Sheddici, hold one truth to be undeniable.

We have our sheds, and the others haven't.

The Roots of Sheddism

Did Boadicea have a shed?

If love is a many splendoured thing and a garden is a lovesome thing (God wot), what is a shed? Someone you know might say 'A shed? It's a shed. That's one, over there'.

Woe is us and lack-a-day. We can only hope that poor souls such as these will pick up this book, feel the tremor of excitement which accompanies that Eureka Moment and, at their leisure, study the mysteries within. Let them learn the dark secrets, previously wrapped in antique riddle and known only to the chosen few.

The roots of international Sheddism can clearly be seen in the Dark Ages, in pre-Norman England and in the language spoken in those days, and the spread of Sheddism through the world has tended to be most noticeable among those virtuous and intellectual populations whose first language is English. Even so, we must ask if there are not traces of sheds, sheddies and possibly even the Sheddici themselves, before that.

Let us turn to the wise words of the late Professor F. J. Haverfield – he of the Chair of Ancient History at the University of Oxford. Here he is, writing of Britain under the Romans. By 'lowlands' he means the region we call the south-east of England – the Home Counties, plus Suffolk, Norfolk, Cambridgeshire and certain areas of the Midlands, being those parts the Romans found the most rewarding and, with a few exceptions, easiest to subdue:

> The lowlands were the scene of civil life. Towns, villages and country houses were their prominent features; troops were hardly seen in them. The uplands of Wales and the north presented another spectacle. Here civil life was almost wholly absent. No country town or country house has been found more than twenty miles north of York or west of Monmouthshire.

The good professor might as well have said that there were no sheds in Wales and the north, except those used as dwelling houses, for a particular level of civilisation is required before the shed can appear as adjunct to basic existence. We can speculate that, in the effete south, some of the wealthier citizens may have had sheds in which to keep scythes, sickles, ploughshares, ox harnesses and tools for mending the spinning wheel, but we cannot see Sheddism existing in any form resembling what we know today.

Of course, there were no habitable lands lower than those lands of Norfolk, home to Queen Boudicca (Boadicea) and the Iceni so, if there were any sheds, they would have been there. It is pleasant to imagine Boudicca and her daughters, busy with their herbal remedies and wild boar paté, banishing husband/father/King Prasutagus to the shed, there to compose songs in praise of the Emperor Nero. 'Prasutagus' roughly translates as the leek-green billy goat, which puts some of our modern parents in their place when it comes to naming children.

Regardless of his name, Prasutagus was a steady type and managed to hold things in balance with the Romans but, when he died, they tried it on. In response, the royal womenfolk rose up, and with them the Iceni, the Trinovantes, the Oritani and very possibly the Sheddici. It started well but finished badly and Sheddism was put back centuries.

With the Romans eventually gone and their decadent civilisation with them, we must wait for a while before the true fathers of Sheddism emerge in history: the Anglo-Saxons.

Do these pictures show the familiar insides of a chaotic shed, or do they have a greater significance? Do they, for example, really illustrate the confused workings of a writer's mind? Answers on the form provided, please, to www.shedblog.co.uk/about.

That which we call a shed

Roughly half of the words we use in modern English have Greek and Latin roots. Possibly a few linguistic remnants of Greek/Latin were left by the Romans but otherwise the whole lot came over as French with the Normans in 1066. In among that half of our language, the Romance half, one word you will not find is 'shed'. That word was in England already, in Anglo-Saxon, and it is in this language that, at last, we find the very essence of sheds, Sheddism and sheddists.

As noted in a previous publication by your correspondent, the Anglo-Saxon word *scead* means shade, shelter or shadow, but we must go deeper than that. You see, there is another word, a similar word, *scēad*, meaning separation or distinction, which in modern English is the shed that is the test of skill and co-operation between shepherd and sheep dog, when required to shed, or separate, a single sheep from the rest of the flock.

In some contexts, *scēad* could also mean discretion or understanding, which are characteristics implicit in Sheddism. *Sceadugeard* (shadowyard) is a shady place. *Scēadwis* (shedwise) means intelligent, sagacious, and that's probably enough Anglo-Saxon for now because you must have the picture.

There, in the old vocabulary, we have the beginnings of threads of meaning, coming from 'shade' and 'separate', which have mingled, and the result is a shed where, intelligent and sagacious as we are, we can shelter from the storm and be shedded from the flock, distinct from racing rodentry.

What's the French for Woodworm?

According to the biographer John Prest, Sir Robert Peel's new police force of 1829 'were not there to carry out sophisticated criminal detective work, but to restrain the thousands of vagrants, thieves, prostitutes and drunks who tried to beg, steal, earn, or expend a living upon the streets of the capital, and to keep order'.

The thin blue line of 'vigorous preventive police' was tasked with 'penning vice back into the rookeries and shielding gentility from coarseness', and so that's what they did. By the middle of that century, with vice well penned, 'the policeman's image was becoming a friendly, neighbourly one, and constables were being called "bobbies" or "peelers" after their founder'.

Peel also stipulated that the men of the new force should be drawn, not from the great, the good and the worthy, as were the magistrates, nor from those inflatedly seeing themselves as such, like the parish beadles, but from the social classes that also produced the aforementioned vagrants, thieves *et cetera*, on the grounds that it takes one to know one.

It must surprise us, therefore, that the young Mick Stephenson, grammar school boy from a good family, should leave a promising financial career in the City of London where, of course, there are no vagrants, thieves, prostitutes or drunks, to join the Essex Constabulary. One of his first experiences in his new office of Constable involved that very species of mankind with which he had been so far unfamiliar, on a Saturday night in Harlow New Town.

He and a couple of other bobbies sorted out the beer-fuelled melee in a reasonably amicable manner, as befits a sporting occasion. In the ensuing peace, one of the civilian combatants asked where was Horizontal.

'Horizontal?' said Mick. 'Who is Horizontal?' The youth named a certain policeman, a man whom Mick regarded as quite elderly, having done at least twenty-five years in the job.

'He's on early turn this week. Why do you call him Horizontal?'

'Because that's how he normally leaves us.'

On another Saturday night, Mick was about to go on duty in his readjusted capacity as traffic cop, when a young lady came into the station. This vision of loveliness clearly could have been Miss Harlow, had she wished, or Miss Essex,

Watch out, there's an antique dealer about.

The cat is called Christmas. It likes going to the pub.

or Miss England come to that, but her wish now was that her car would go. It started all right, and it went into gear all right, but it wouldn't go anywhere.

Had the person requesting police help been a fat, ugly, hairy, tattooed, toothless and hygienically-challenged middle-aged male, Mick would also have offered to take him to the troubled vehicle in his police car, and three other officers would likewise have volunteered to assist in this puzzling work. As it happened, the fragrant beauty, dressed as she was for an exciting evening, was accompanied by those four policemen and conveyed with flashing lights to where her car, a brand new three-litre Ford Capri, was found to be standing, wheel-less, on four piles of bricks.

All that is in the past now. Mick has retired from the force and keeps himself busy in his shed on charitable enterprises, the main one being dealing in rustic French antique tables. He makes regular trips to remote districts of rural France where he buys old tables in poor condition at generously inflated prices, restores them to perfection, and sells them on eBay, often at a loss. As he says, he just likes helping people out. http://stores.ebay.co.uk/Saffron-Antiques.

The French for woodworm, by the way, is *ver du bois*.

TRUE OR FALSE?

Would you rather be a Remiser?

Do the French really have a word that means 'shed' as we mean it in English? Could the Anglo-Saxons have adopted the words the Normans used? Could we have become, for instance, remisers instead of sheddies?

One translation of *la remise* is the shed, fair enough, but perhaps more in the sense of somewhere to put things, such as paraphernalia (from the Latin *parapherna*, the separate possessions of a married woman). *Remise* is from the verb *remettre*, to remit or put back, but which can also mean to replay.

Quand est-ce qu'on remet ça dans la remise? is 'When are we going to do it again in the shed?'

You can also say *l'abri*, the shed, but generally meaning the shelter, with undertones of safety from the pressing world. The verb *abriter* means to shelter, to shield from. *L'abri antiatomique/antinucléaire* is fallout shelter, *l'abri fiscal* is tax haven, and *l'abri de jardin* is more gazebo or summerhouse than garden shed. *L'abri de chantier*, literally the shelter of the building site, could be used to mean a shed where work is the main intention.

The Latin root of *abri is apricus/apricum* which – now listen to this – means the exact opposite of shed. It means to lie uncovered and unsheltered, especially in a sunny place. So that must be why we're Sheddists and not Apricots.

Tea, Anyone?

The Low House in Laxfield, Suffolk, is one of the very few pubs left in Britain that has no bar-counter. You go in the tap room at the back. Beer drinkers survey the array of barrels and request whatever takes their fancy, drawn straight from the barrel, while others can order whatever you usually have.

As if that were not a rare enough circumstance, there is no pool table, no piped music, no coin-in-the-slot of any kind, no television large or small. Dogs are welcomed and given a biscuit.

The landlady is Linda Bower, and her connections with the pub go back to Victorian times. Her great-grandfather Arthur Felgate, the village blacksmith, took over The King's Head, which is the Low House's proper name, around 1882 as the tenant of Etheridge's Brewery of Eye, which became Fisher's Brewery in 1874. Adnams of Southwold, then one of almost 10,000 independent brewers in Britain, bought it in 1904.

Linda's great-granddad ran it until he died in 1943, then his son Stephen, Linda's grandfather, assumed command. After he died the pub went through several ownerships and some very difficult times. Adnams sold it. In 2001 – by which time they were one of only fifty independent brewers in Britain – they bought it again, and Linda's family connection was re-established when she took it on with her very own grumpy old man, Bob.

By 2010 they were running curry nights, pie and mash nights, Thai/Italian/ Hungarian nights, Shakespeare in the garden, Morris dancers, folk singers, petanque matches, beer festivals, veteran car rallies, horse-drawn carriage rides, but Linda thought there was still something missing. So she bought a shed.

We present Linda Bower, Queen of Teas, home-baked sconer, whipper of cream, darling of Darjeeling, and her shed.

TRUE OR FALSE?

Sheds in Poetry

Readers are invited to compose the poem 'Ode to a Shed' or 'Sonnet on a Shed', or 'Sonnet in a Shed', because, despite the mellow fruitfulness of the subject and the possibility of daffodils outside, established poets have so far signally failed to expose the heart of the matter:

> At night returning, every labour sped,
> He sits him down, the monarch of a shed;
> Smiles by his cheerful fire, and round surveys
> His children's looks, that brighten at the blaze;
> While his lov'd partner, boastful of her hoard,
> Displays her cleanly platter on the board.

The Traveller, **Oliver Goldsmith,** *1764*

Children? Lov'd partner? Great Scott, surely the whole idea is to get away from children and partners, lov'd or not lov'd. Poor old Goldsmith was clearly lost on sheds and he's by no means the only one, although Andrew Marvell (1621–1678) wasn't so far off the button in his poem *The Garden* with his famous line 'A green thought in a green shed'.

Rudyard Kipling (1865 – 1936) said something similar in his poem *The Glory of the Garden*:

> Our England is a garden, and such gardens are not fed
> By singing:- 'Oh, how beautiful!' and sitting in the shed.

The question 'Why a shed?' is a difficult one, we know, and as hard for poetry to answer as it is to pin down the exact meaning of the question in the first place. If we doubted that, the puzzling nature of Rupert Brooke's reference to it should make us feel better, while not actually explaining anything. This is in *The Old Vicarage, Grantchester*, the same poem that has that bit about the church clock at ten to three and is there honey still for tea:

> And oft between the boughs is seen
> The sly shed of a Rural Dean.

Come again? Make of that what you will, but perhaps the most revealing truth about Sheddism is to be found, not in a poem by a man but one by a woman. Read it. You'll see what she's getting at. Obviously the word 'my' is missing between 'to' and 'shed' but that's poetry for you:

> O! haste to shed the sovereign balm,
> My shatter'd nerves new string;
> And for my guest, serenely calm,
> The nymph Indifference bring.

Floruit, **Mrs Greville,** *1753*

No Microwave in Shed

It used to be part of the verbal contract between worker and master on a certain farm, in the valley of the river Eden, Westmorland, now called Cumbria, that salmon would be served to the men no more than three times a week. Alas for those horny-handed sons of toil, there was no such mention of brisket on the bone and so that, with heaps of potatoes and cabbage, plus Mrs Wills's unique gravy, was what they got in the 1930s, 40s and 50s, on the four non-salmon days, and more often when the fish weren't running.

One young lad, son of the regular cowman, came to work on his first day and sat down to his dinner at twelve o'clock with the others. He was issued with a wooden bowl about the size of a two-pint pudding basin, a knife and a spoon, and watched with some concern as Mrs Wills, the master's wife, ladled a pint or so of green liquid into each man's bowl.

'There's two sorts of broth in the world, son,' whispered his father. 'Green broth. And brown broth. Today, it's green broth.'

In silence, they set to and ate their broth. Meanwhile, Mrs Wills was hacking lumps off a huge piece of roast cow, and rattling various blackened pots and pans which stood on the hob of the range or hung on a crane over the fire. When the broth was gone, she went around the table with those comestibles already mentioned – brisket of beef, spuds, cabbage, gravy – filling the bowls to the top.

Halfway down his bowl, the lad was flagging. Two thirds of the way down and he could eat no more. His father said nothing. The other men noticed and likewise said nothing as each cleaned up his last drop of Mrs Wills's gravy.

Round she came again, with suet pudding and custard, and to the boy first. On top of his uneaten meat and veg she sloshed, with a mighty slosh, a goodly portion of pud and a ladleful of custard. The message in her heavily-accented sloshing was clear. Compared to the fate in store for those foolish boys who did not eat all their dinner, hell's fires would be as the touch of a butterfly's wing.

The men, including father, were enjoying the moment very much but, in that northern way, not showing it by so much as a lip twitch. They finished their puddings and went back to work. The boy had to stay until his was all gone too.

The answer, his father told him, was to work harder, then he'd be hungrier.

This is the old cabin, one of the many sheds with which your correspondent was endowed when purchasing said farm in Westmorland. Here Mrs Wills used to cook daily for the men, except Sundays, and sometimes there would be a dozen of them. When Mr Wills, thinking only of the ease and comfort of his wife, had a modern, coal-fired Rayburn stove installed in the house, Mrs Wills refused to use it, preferring her old range in the cabin.

This was one of the new uses to which the cabin shed was put. We were still feeding the hungry but nothing was ever left.

Heavenly sheds at night are falling – the cabin is second from the left, the one with the chimney. Beyond that is an open log shed, and a laundry shed with wash copper set in brick. In use, a fire was lit beneath and there was a tap to let the used water out to run down the shed floor and into the yard.

Beyond, the square building is the dairy. That had two-inch thick pine shelves for the butter and cheese, and a slate-lined pit in the floor, about twelve feet by eight and three feet deep, where the milk churns could stand to keep cool.

Nearest is the smithy, part of which fell down the night we just happened to park the car somewhere else.

Meek Geek Speaks: Seeks Sneakery

The Wileys live near Portsmouth, New Hampshire, famous old harbour town on the estuary of the Piscataqua River and location of one of the oldest timber-framed sheds in the USA, the Richard Jackson house. Mr Jackson was a woodworker as well as a farmer and seaman, and he built the beginnings of the house out of wood in 1664.

Rob Wiley is neither farmer nor seadog, but a self-confessed 'mild-mannered computer geek', which is how he earns his living by day. For evidence of his abilities, one need only look at his wife Laurie's very slick website, http://handymancraftywoman.com. The tagline on it, 'So many home projects, so little time', gives the clue about this family, forever improving the nest.

Built by someone with the same high standards as Rob Wiley, this is the Jackson house, originally a small shed we can surmise, begun in 1664 and still there, near Portsmouth, New Hampshire. It's one of the oldest sheds in the USA, developed over the years into a much larger house when the warmth of the cattle in the downstairs reception room was more important than the smell. Illustration by Sue Thorburn

The need to have a bolt-hole outside the nest, whether derived from deep-seated sheddish motivations or not, was described logically, woodworking man to wife, as a storage measure. Somewhere was required to put the lawnmower, the snow-blower (they have hard winters there) and the generator (they have power cuts in the hard winters). Indeterminate conversations took place over a year, during which time several other handy projects rose to the top of the list and were completed.

The debate centred around the interesting fact that they already had a cellar and a garage, and the snow-blower, mower and generator, also each and every tool, device, machine, contrivance, labour saver, implement and instrument whatsoever, were all safely stowed therein or elsewhere on the property. A view through the window onto the garden did not reveal piles of valued items left, willy nilly, to deteriorate. When mowing the lawn with the previously mentioned lawnmower, one did not have to keep moving miscellaneous objects out of the way. In sum, they didn't need any more storage space.

Rob's response was that he was looking to the future. Laurie quoted Pickford's Law, which states: 'The amount of stuff expands to fill the space available.'

There are a million reasons, spoken and unspoken, for having a shed, but there is not a single, solid, irrefutable argument against having one, unless

That, as they say in America, is some kind of shed.

Purely for storage.

there is nowhere to put it. An area twelve feet by eight was not difficult to find chez Wiley and so, rejecting the temptations of prefabricated models, Rob followed the pioneering spirit of Richard Jackson by designing and building his shed. As can be seen from the pictures, it is a substantial construction, serviceable as living quarters should the need arise.

During the build, the summer sun beat down on Rob, while Laurie supplied him with lemonade. Winter was months away. Come the autumn, the shed would open for business, and very soon the snow blower, generator, lawnmower and various other gear would fill it, and he would need another for himself.

TRUE OR FALSE?

Butchery in the Roman Shed

Continuing our researches into the dim and distant, we find that the Latin word for a plank is *tabula*, and for a hut or shed made out of planks, *taberna*. In Ancient Rome, if an oik or peasant had a taberna, he would not treat it as an addition to life but rather would live in it and be grateful for it. Or, he might work in it. The word taberna, from which we get tavern of course, often meant a small shop or workshop, as is made clear in this excerpt from Livy's *History of Rome* (no stone unturned where sheds are concerned):

'He (her father, Lucius Verginius) draws the girl and the nurse aside to the sheds near the temple of Cloacina, which now go by the name of the new sheds: and there snatching up a knife from a butcher…he then transfixes the girl's breast.'

So, you see, one of the new sheds was a butcher's shop. As for the poor girl, she was a beauteous but lower-class maiden called Verginia, daughter of the centurion Lucius, promised in marriage to another ordinary sort of a chap. However, a rich and powerful fellow, one of the rulers of Rome called Appius Claudius Crassus, lusted after her but couldn't get anywhere, and so he had had her taken on her way to school:

> … as she was coming into the forum, for there in the sheds the literary schools were held; calling her the daughter of his slave and a slave herself.

After being thus described in public, Verginia's future did not look rosy. As a slave, she would be sold into prostitution. Rather than that, her father borrowed the butcher's knife, without asking.

This happened around 450 BC. The Romans had got rid of their kings fifty years before and founded a republic, but Appius seemed to be harking back to the bad old days of power abuse. The result was a popular revolution, with Appius and his aristocratic mates all sacked from office and the republic reinstalled. And all because there was a shed nearby.

Green Beryl Only Eats Fish

Sapphire is the last of the eel catchers, Scott wants to be an explorer (and with a name like that he should be), Pearl is a strange old man with a parrot and, as we say, Green Beryl is a fishy sort of a character. If you've never seen Eel Island on the telly, you can catch up at www.eelisland.co.uk and listen to some of Jon Goddard's haunting, atmospheric music.

He also wrote the score for Stephen Fry's reading of the Little Tim stories by Edward Ardizzone, in which our hero – much shipwrecked and often wet – battles through his adventures accompanied by six different sorts of storm music.

That this kind of thing would be Jon's life was apparent from an early age. After trying to play a saxophone that was bigger than he was, he switched to guitar and was soon mixed up in an avant garde rock band. As if that were not bad enough, he went to art college and formed a modern jazz trio.

Top left is the Canary Islands timple, featured on Jon Goddard's album Swell, *next to a 1920s five-string banjo which has a much softer tone than the brash modern ones. The square neck resonator at the front is played on the lap with a steel slide, country style. The acoustic guitar to the left is Nashville tuned, with the four bass strings an octave up, and behind is a 1960s Japanese semi-acoustic in quasi-baritone tuning.*

Audio books, shows in the theatre, telly ads, telly programmes, rock and roll bands in pubs, it's all the same to Jon, and it's so much easier now he has moved his studio from the spare bedroom to the conservatory to the shed, out there at the end of the garden, surrounded by miles and miles of the flattest bit of Suffolk. He's also surrounded by eleven acoustic guitars, being two resonators, two nylon-strung, four steel-strung, two parlour guitars and one F-hole jazz guitar, and six electric guitars.

Parlour guitars look small to modern eyes but a hundred years ago they were the norm and were/are quite loud enough for intimate settings. They're coming back into fashion, too, in both parlor/parlour method, an American finger-style way of playing without plectrum, and with luthiers who are making them in larger numbers. (Luthier, pron. looty-ay, one who makes lutes and hence one who makes stringed instruments played with the fingers. Again, *Remember When* does its bit for Scrabble players).

In case guitars get boring, Jon has an old five-string banjo, a banjolin, a ukulele, a mandolin, and a timple (Tim-play – Canary Islands five-string instrument similar to a ukulele). He doesn't have a lyre or a lute, but would like one of each, and there's an antique German piano with gilt lion heads inside where only the piano tuner will ever see them, a button accordion, alto sax, violin, hand drums,

Here's Jon on his Japanese semi-accoustic. Quasi-baritone tuning means the top four strings are an octave down but the two bass strings are normal, and if you want to know why, ask someone from Nashville, because there they do just t'opposite.

mouth organs, and a flute that daughter Anja plays. Son Hunter, like the Owl to the Pussycat, also sings to a small guitar, but father Jon obviously hopes that his offspring will become accountants or solicitors rather than musicians.

See also www.jongoddard.co.uk and Amazon etc for his album *Swell*.

TRUE OR FALSE?

Sheds and sex

Philosophers may try to dissect and make rational an activity which cannot be so categorised. Poets may rant and gibber with their oxymorons, synecdoches and architraves. Scientists may postulate that, just as there is no difference between genetically modified sprouting broccoli bought in a supermarket, versus your own broccoli fresh from the garden, so there is no difference between shedfulness and shedlessness.

If Sheddism is spiritual, a choice made freely by the finer instruments of our being, that is, those characteristics which set us aside from the beasts of

the field, why is it so strongly associated with men? Do not women have these same finer spiritual instruments?

The answer, dear reader, used to look like no. In days gone by, the ladies, bless them, were simply not in the shed, but now we have Sheddistes in the Congregation.

John Knox issued his First Blast of the Trumpet against The Monstrous Regiment of Women in 1558, almost 200 years before Mrs Greville wrote her poem featuring the shed as sovereign balm (see p. 21). Knox, a troublemaker if ever there was one, believed that lads were forced into their sheds by lasses waving never-ending lists of man-things to do. He, simple soul, did not realise that men constructed their hideaways and escaped to them of their own volition, leaving her indoors where she wanted to be, and where she believed she had the better of it.

That was ages ago. As Mr Neville 'Noddy' Holder MBE and the young gentlemen of the musical ensemble Slade once put it, Mama, Mama, we're all crazy now.

I Don't Mind If I Do

Designed and built by Tim McNeill and voted Shed of the Year 2008, the Rugby Pub can be described in several ways. For example, it has eight roof lights in an octagonal roof, double doors opening as one entrance, and a fifteen-foot fully fitted bar with storage under, including three fridges. It has blinds to the windows and roof lights, a ceiling fan, a sink with running water, and it is comfortably furnished with sea grass matting on the floor and a hammock handily slung. Recent design mods include a cat flap.

Since this picture was taken of Tim McNeill's pub shed, a clematis has draped itself, triffid-like, over the roof lights, thus increasing those special senses of shade and separation of which we wrote earlier. Also a wren has built its nest, not – as Edward Lear would have it – in Tim's beard but in his eaves.

You might wonder, if you have very good eyesight, why an optic bearing labels for White Horse whisky and Remy Martin brandy in fact supports a bottle of Famous Grouse, or, indeed, why Bacardi is announced by the legend J & B Rare. Such wondering would be a foolish waste of time, and the suggestion instead is that you contemplate a bottle of Sneck Lifter by Jennings of Cockermouth. Sneck, by the way, for anyone unfamiliar with northern English and Scots dialect words, is not a vulgar euphemism but rather a door latch or, more specifically, that part which operates or lifts the mechanism of the type of fastening commonly called a Suffolk latch. Confused? Well, yes, because Sneck Lifter would therefore appear to be tautological, and it's probably from an old Dutch word related to snack and snatch. So, even in a small, private pub, you can still hear a lot of old rubbish talked, just as you can in a normal one.

Tim also describes it as his first attempt at creating anything significant, from which we must infer that he means anything inanimate, since it was his daughter who named the shed by giving him a Rugby Pub sign for Christmas, he having been a rugger bugger all his life.

It has no telephone (mobiles forbidden on pain of death), no television receiver, no wireless telegraph, and so no electronic interruptions to the liquid refreshment, of which there is no shortage. This results in no inclination and no need to go anywhere else.

Occasionally there is a supply of namesake Ray McNeill's beer from the microbrewery in Brattleboro, Vermont, USA. Brewer Ray does ten beers. McNeill's ESB is 'dry with a deep nose of grapefruit'. Champ Ale is 5.5% with 'very high drinkability'. Dead Horse IPA 'gives a deep bow to British IPAs' and has 'strong notes of butter'. Tim says the IPA is pretty good, and McNeill's beers have won various American awards but, being American, the beers tend to be sweeter. So, to increase drinkability to medium or high, buttered horses need to be served cold.

More likely, Tim's guests will find him dispensing pints of an English bitter such as Mauldon's Mole Trap or Silver Adder, session beers from the Sudbury brewery which is fairly local to him. Nothing is for sale, by the way, so thirsty Revenue persons are welcome.

Had such guests come along in the early days, they would have found Tim keeping the old-fashioned Sunday lunchtime hours of twelve to two, but now drinking in the Rugby Pub is by appointment only, which might entail Madame running with urgent messages across the garden to the shed, where Tim says he is quite often to be found.

TRUE OR FALSE?

Life Choices

So you've had a bad day. Nothing's gone right. Well, you have a number of options. For example, you could have a bath with aromatic oils, a cup of ginseng tea and half an hour's transcendental meditation, followed by a funny cigarette while listening to a recording of the poems of Jack Kerouac.

Or, you could go down the off licence, kit yourself out with a half dozen of Old Shagnasty, and stagger round the corner to the Moti Mahal. There, you could order a take-away of popadoms with lime and garlic pickle, mutton vindaloo, chicken Bangalore phall, paratha and chilli channa, and take the whole lot back to your shed.

Which is it to be?

Mailman, Bring Me No More Blues

In a world where everyone seems set on computerising everything, a word of warning issues forth from a shed in Essex. Here, in that shed, are resting the only remnants of what was possibly the maddest attempt at computerisation ever conceived, a system with no sensible purpose that could be divined by anyone other than a member of post-office management seduced by the glitter of technology.

Imagine yourself, for a moment, as a postman or postwoman in Northampton in the late 1990s. You are in your van, doing your collection rounds. There are road works, it's snowing, there is a student demo, a bus has broken down in the high street, and a swarm of bees is terrorising the fruit and veg stall on the market (it sometimes snows in the summer in Northampton). Despite all of this, you get to your next pillar box only six minutes after the designated

Steve Knight is fascinated by the differences between post boxes.

collection time. Alas, you cannot open the box. The computer within has decided that you are not the authorised collector, because you were not there a minute ago.

The box will not open to your 'Intellikey' until next time around, assuming you get there within five minutes either side of the given time, and assuming the batteries have not run out, in which case the machine will have forgotten all about you and your programmable key and you will have to call in a locksmith with a drill, cold chisel and four-pound hammer. Heavy rain also can bring about this result.

After a short while, and a massive increase in sick notes due to nervous breakdowns in post collectors, the utter nincompoopery of this experiment will be realised and the whole business quietly withdrawn.

To learn about such marvels, and a great deal else besides of a postal nature, you must go to a shed, to wit, the Colne Valley Postal History Museum in Halstead, Essex. The weather-susceptible exhibits, such as a Victorian postman's shako hat, donated by someone whose great-grandfather wore it to work, are kept inside it, floor area 56 square feet. No room there, then, for the hundred pillar boxes and one telephone box, but there are nineteen stamp machines and all sorts of memorabilia including more telephone stuff and, in a departure from the GPO, some rare and lovely examples of those landscape prints you used to see in railway carriages when they had compartments.

One man stands behind all this, Steve Knight who, in his own words, 'started collecting post boxes…having been fascinated by the differences between them for many years'.

Fascinations of this type are not explicable by psychologists or any other ologists, but we know they are a natural, latent part of the inclination to Sheddism which, like the tiny seed of the wild Bee Orchid, has all the potential for astonishing beauty within a speck of dust but needs the luck of circumstance to set the process going.

Steve was a stamp collector as a boy, so there's a bit of a postal link there, but his luck of circumstance came at an antiques fair where he saw a brilliant red light in the shape of a lamp box (small mailbox found mostly in rural districts, often fixed to a post, pole or street lamp, hence the name). It was not an especially rare one – ERII – but for £100 with a working lock it seemed irresistible.

The next one Steve saw was £200, which implied a substantial profit for the dealer, so he wrote to head offices in all the postal towns of East Anglia, and Cambridge came up with two wall boxes (like lamp boxes but set in a wall) at £100 each. By this time, retreat was impossible, which is why Steve has, in his shed, cap badges, uniforms, telegram forms, water jugs, fire extinguishers, collection plates, direction signs, scales, string, scissors, knives, pencils, proper pens with ink wells, stained glass, stamp moistening pads, stamps, lamps, cramps and old hats – anything and everything connected to the magic three letters: G P O, General Post Office, as was in the charge of the Postmaster General, when it was believed that the telephone and postal services were sisters.

Steve's shed is electrified, telephoned and broadbanded and can simulate a real Post Office from any period of the last half-century, and you can visit at any reasonable time by appointment. Steve loves it when groups of retired Royal Mail staff come round, saying 'Oh, yes, that was for such-and-such', and 'We used to hate those'. There are open days, and school visits – school children are enthralled by the stamp vending machines using £sd coinage. They've never seen a threepenny bit before, and they can usually get into the Victorian uniforms that are too small for most modern adults. Steve's wife is a teacher and he has plenty of ex-GPO mates, so experts are always on hand. Go to www. cvphm.org or call 01787 474412.

They have between three and four hundred visitors now, in an average year. And once upon a time, a small boy started collecting stamps.

Most of the stuff Steve Knight gets is in great need of restoration, especially those post boxes that have had fireworks exploded inside them, and he has a team of expert mates who help him do that. Perhaps what many letter posters don't realise is just how much of the pillar box is below ground, and how heavy they are.

Ashram in Somerset

A round 300 AD, in India there lived a wise man called Patanjali. He devised a system for calming the jarring vibrations of the *chitta*, the consciousness, thus bringing balance and harmony between body and soul, and he set out his system of *asana* (posture) and *pranayama* (breathing) techniques in 196 *sutra* (erudite and pithy sayings), leading to *Samadhi*, the state of self-realisation. Yes, he'd described yoga.

Many years later, in 1972 AD to be precise, Marian Turner was in a queue to register for Spanish evening classes at the local tech but, by the time she got to the front, Spanish was full, likewise double-entry book-keeping and putting ships in bottles. In fact, yoga was the only course left, so she joined that.

The Hindu goddess Kali, variously seen as the timelord, a goddess of destruction and the mother of all, stands on her consort Shiva, himself a complex figure sometimes seen as the god of gods. The severed head that Kali carries in one of her hands represents the overweening spirit of mankind which must be conquered by divine understanding. All the other heads on her scarf are the equivalent of rosary beads, for prayers.

That Marian Turner should have this redoubtable presence in her shed indicates perhaps more than she realised (see below).

Fate or accident? Whatever it was, it soon became apparent that there was a problem at home with finding a tranquil space on the floor to practise, even though she's only five feet tall. The next fateful accident was coming across a shed while out buying some Fiery Jack and a packet of aspirins for her husband Jeff, whose brief attempt at yoga accompaniment had come to a painful end.

The octagonal construction of the discovered shed seemed to Marian to echo somehow the intricacies of yoga, and she felt sufficiently versed in the art to be able to give up her lessons at ten quid a time. Her shed-as-ashram would soon pay for itself.

Every morning, Marian goes to her shed, lies on her mat, and turns on the CD player to hear the instructions of her guru, 92-year-old yoga legend B.K.S. Iyengar, whose inventions of 'wooden gadgets, belts and ropes' have helped open up the world of yoga to those westerners with less flexible bodies, or 'ordinary human beings' as he calls them.

In her shed, lined with brilliantly-colourful Indian tapestries, Marian searches daily for mental peace, emotional equanimity and clarity of mind or, as she puts it in her own words, it helps keep me healthy.

TRUE OR FALSE?

Are You of the Faith?

Sir Arthur Mangle in *Primitive Cultures of the British Isles* proposes 'a belief in spiritual beings' as a minimum qualification for a Sheddist. However, Professor Tattington-Carver subsequently made clear, in his series of lectures on BBC Radio Three, that ritual is in fact primary in Sheddism, while dogma and myth are secondary.

In a Small Hotel, by a Wishing Well

Victoria Corcoran and Craig Hailes's shed looks like a normal summerhouse – a rather nice big one, admittedly, with verandah – but normal. Ah, but normal summerhouses, even in Liverpool, do not have air conditioning, CCTV, lighting sensors, alarms, piped music and eighteen bedrooms, each convertible to a suite by the addition of a run.

These are not bedrooms in the B&B/hotel sense. The guests are not people but small animals, temporarily homeless while their usual keepers are on holiday or otherwise engaged. Birds, chinchillas, mice, rats, hamsters, tortoises, rabbits, gerbils, guinea pigs – the full range of household pets that are not cats or dogs are given VIP treatment in the hotel shed. Exceptions are parrots, being too noisy; snakes, which may regard the other guests as lunch; and ferrets. Ferrets emit a smell, an aura almost, which gives the heebie-jeebies to rabbits and other small mammals, so that they suffer from what the psychologists call 'floating anxiety'.

Wot? No goldfish?

All the animals listen through the day to Smooth FM.

Here is a message from a lady called Denise: 'Our guinea pig Patch spent his summer holiday at the Small Animal Hotel. We could see him on Facebook and he was loving all the attention he was getting. Patch is looking forward to his next holiday.'

Denise, guinea pigs do not look forward to things. They take life as it comes. You see … oh, never mind. Love to Patch.

The rabbit and guinea-pig pamper session goes like this. Shampoo. Leave on for three minutes, and rinse. Follow with conditioner, to de-tangle and leave those split ends soft and something or other. Rinse. Blow-dry and comb. Because you're worth it.

Interesting, but it's not a shed

The bearded dragon, *Poggona vitticeps*, originates from the arid regions of central Australia but is captive-bred worldwide for the pet trade. It is a fairly demanding guest at the hotel shed, needing carefully regulated tank temperatures and live grasshoppers for dinner. Male dragons grow to about two feet long including tail, but females are smaller. They do a lot of head bobbing and a certain amount of hand signalling to other dragons, but otherwise list their activities as 'lying in the sun' and 'sleeping in my burrow'.

There Stood a Log Cabin Made of Earth and Wood

Johnny B. Goode's cabin was way down in Louisiana but this one, built by country boy and Eagle Scout Michael Despeaux, is high up in the Appalachian Mountains, which include the Great Smoky Mountains and the Blue Ridge Mountains, and lots of other mountains. Michael's patch, in a small valley or 'holler' as he calls it, is in North Carolina, where run some of the world's most challenging rivers for white-water canoeists. Indeed, Michael is one of these, and it was while hurtling down the notorious Green River that he tore his rotator cuff (shoulder muscles), leaving him up his holler without recourse to his paddle, and in need of a project.

Way back up in the woods among the evergreens.

Another Anglo-Saxon word: adesa – *adze.*

There are and have been many DIY shed building projects but few can equal this one. Although Michael is a university graduate (in English, unlike Johnny B who never ever learned to read and write so well), he didn't really know the first thing about building log cabins, not that such a lack of know-how made him hesitate. The first thing, in fact, is posts or foundation piles sunk into the ground. These were Black Locust wood, a hard, heavy, naturally rot-resistant timber that grows freely in those parts, and the same wood was used for the foundation beams.

Interesting, but it's not a shed

A crosscut saw, for sawing across the grain of green hardwood, has two kinds of teeth. Between pairs of conventionally shaped cutting teeth are single 'rakers', double-pointed teeth meant to pull the sawdust out of the cut. These, Michael Despeaux says, should be perhaps 1/1200th of an inch shorter than the cutter teeth. Some sawyers tap the two points of each raker, bending the edge over, lengthways to the saw, giving them a sort of chisel angle so that they pull more shavings out of the cut. The term for a tool used for bending cold metal is a swage, pronounced 'swedge', hence this process is called swaging the rakers.

Michael and friends had chainsaws, of course, but the old technology of drawknife, adze, hatchet and slick (very big chisel) appealed more. Floor joists went across the beams, pine and oak planks across the joists for the floor, and now for the walls.

We should point out at this juncture that logs, piles and beams all came from trees felled by Michael and pals. This was ultimate DIY. Trees felled, trunks stripped, naked logs notched to lock together. The naked logs were poplar trees, debarked while still wet from felling, with a specialised drawknife called a bark spud. This extremely keen implement needed very careful handling.

The bark spud, says Michael, has a long, spoon-like curved blade, except unlike a spoon it's flat across the width, not concave. This curvature slides under the bark and along the roundness of the tree trunk, from side to side. It has rounded, sharp corners transitioning from the flat head of the blade to the sides, which are also sharp. Getting under the bark requires digging these corners in between it and the wood and gently rocking the tool until it slips into that space.

That is assuming you have cut your tree down in the first place, and it hasn't rolled down the hill and over a cliff. A tree rarely falls on its feller, incidentally. The more likely injury, almost always serious and sometimes fatal, comes from the falling tree losing a branch, or knocking one off a neighbour as it falls, which can be the equivalent of a javelin thrown from on high.

Once the building was up and its tin roof was on, the problem had to be faced of how to fill in the gaps between the logs, called chinking. Michael

tried modern expanding foam but hated it. Cement was not right either. An expert advised a mix of clay and sand with horse manure or, as Chuck Berry describes it, earth. At the time of writing, with winter being allowed to air-condition the logs into stability, this remains an unresolved matter.

Michael started in March 2010 and reckoned a year would do it, including seasoning for the logs, made from trees felled by himself and friends from the land around the site. They celebrated completion of the basic structure with a Kayakerator* full of craft IPA, brewed by Sean of the Tuckaseegee Brewing Cooperative, who has a PhD in microbiology and a knack for growing hops. The Kayakerator will make frequent visits, says Michael. Much of the time, the Coldholler Cabin will be a playground for children, but there'll always be a locked up bottle of good peaty single malt there to accommodate adult visitors. (*Kayakerator – beer dispenser shaped like a kayak, for obvious reasons).

TRUE OR FALSE?

After you've had your friends round for a few drinks and you're left alone in the shed, lie down on the couch. Let your thoughts wander. Relax. Soon you will be progressing through the various stages of the First Phase of Meditation: the haze, the doze, the snooze, the restful sleep.

Next, you will move into the two stages of the Second Phase: the waking up, and the strong desire for a bacon sandwich with brown sauce.

Birdowse Man of Stockport

Being an ex building surveyor, works study officer and estate manager, a flat-pack shed held no terrors for Mike Durcan, even though it came as individual planks and a million little bits, not prefabricated into handy chunks. He found that the instructions seemed to refer to a previous model, or perhaps to another kind of shed altogether, which will be an experience familiar to anyone who has tried to assemble kitchen units. But, Mike read between the lines and did the job.

The first task, with his new, three and a half metres square Swiss cottage completed, was to move in all his treasures. That these should include robots, several different versions of Monopoly and a Tony the Tiger (Frosties. They're

The annexe to the right of the Swiss cottage is the original, smaller shed, now used for simple gardening purposes.

Gr-r-r-reat!) should come as a surprise to nobody. Next came the woodburner and, gradually, that feeling of peace and contentment which is the aim of so many of us. He even moved in for a while, so he could awake to the sounds of blackbirds scrabbling about on the roof.

'It's amazing what it does for your soul,' says Mike. 'I could feel stress leaking away. Everything was under my own control.'

Retired from work and seeking something kind of organic, he looked at a piece of wood and saw in it a nesting box. He studied the basic requirements of nesting boxes as evidenced by the proprietary ones in his garden, and the idea was confirmed. His box turned out quite unlike any nesting box he had ever seen, which encouraged him to make another, which also turned out nice again.

Nesting boxes, or birdowses as he called them, became his occupation. He's a quick and imaginative worker. Every owse was different from the last. His partner Joanne said he should sell them, but he felt too attached. He made more. Soon, he had over a hundred. His friends also said he should sell them but he knew, like all craft workers, that you never get your time and effort back in the price people will pay for something handmade.

So he made yet more. It got to the point where he had a choice. Buy another shed to put them in, or sell some to make room. In fact, he's done both. See picture overleaf and www.birdowse.co.uk.

Ours is a nice owse, ours is.

Interesting, but it's not a shed

This is one of those philosophical questions, like 'Can fairies get through cat flaps?' or 'Why is a mouse when it spins?' It may even be metaphysical,

which is to say it could concern that branch of speculation which deals with the first principles of things.

We have to ask ourselves, can a species other than *Homo sapiens* have a shed? Clearly, these small buildings made by Mike Durcan meet some of the normal criteria but their primary purpose is residential which, at least in some minds, disqualifies them. We must also consider the matter of flight. For most of us, the shed is our refuge, to which we fly as often as we can. The blue tits using these sheds, if they are such, have but a single plan: to get away from them as soon as their families are self-sufficient.

So, on balance, and despite any charm and promises of a secret garden, this correspondent at any rate will reluctantly have to vote against.

Interesting, but it's still not a shed

On the Stockport Road, the old shop offers sweets from tiny jars and proclaims the virtues of Doctor Carrot, the Children's Best Friend. We don't expect the birds, which will fly in and out of the open upstairs window, to appreciate the craftsmanship and humour, but we do. Mike Durcan, you are hereby declared a Shed Genius (special title carrying no observable benefits whatsoever).

Graphical Glamour in the Shed

When Nicola Brown of Shrewsbury went up to university to study graphic design, she needed a studio. There wasn't really room in the house, and an extension looked far too expensive, and then she thought 'Shed!' Ones that were big enough also seemed too much money until boyfriend's mother saw a second-hand one for £200.

Boyfriend's father, brother-in-law, and her own dad and brother put the shed up. Boyfriend wired it for heat, light, computer and so on, and Nicola did the insulation, lining and decorating, and there she was.

Alone, the artist worked on her degree course and final show for eighteen months, never out of the shed, and when she closed the door, after her finals, she didn't think she'd be going back in.

It's always ten past ten in Nicola's shed.

Gradually, the shed lost its identity. It became a mere shelter for strimmers, a dumping ground for garden forks, *Hozelock* sprayers and half-empty packets of *Miracle-Gro*, while Nicola worked as a freelance in the nice warm offices of design agencies.

And then she thought 'Business!', cleared out the rubbish and made it all lovely again (for those of you looking at the pictures in black and white, it's mostly pink inside). Nicola set up on her own account as Creative Director of In The Shed. At first, persons answering the telephone at potential clients' premises were a little bemused by the opening gambit: 'Hello, I'm Nicola Brown from In The Shed', but she got over that and it became quite a selling point.

The firm does logo and stationery design, leaflets, brochures, packaging, exhibitions, marketing material, magazines and websites. Nicola says 'We are In The Shed because we love it. It's where so many great ideas happen, which is why our clients love it too.'

The plan is to expand, hire staff, become a bigger agency, but to keep the shed idea. A much bigger shed? The same shed with extensions? High tech barn? An underground complex with the same shed above as entrance hall? These are points yet to be decided. Meanwhile, Nicola is back in there, in the shed, every day, working for her dream. See how she's doing on www.in-theshed.co.uk.

TRUE OR FALSE?

Coughs and Sneezes, Shed Diseases

Charles Porter, MD, BSc, MRCP, late Medical Officer of Health to the Metropolitan Borough of St Marylebone, had this to say:

'The natural, perhaps even the ideal, life is that which is lived out of doors. The reasons which led the caveman to seek a cave and other prehistoric peoples to construct homes of leaves and branches, staves and mud and stones and so on, are the same, to all intents and purposes, as those that drive the moderns into their mansions, their flats, their cottages, or their tenements of one or two rooms.

'Of all the reasons the chief is protection: protection from the elements, which burn or freeze or drown: protection from foes who rob or wound or kill: protection from friends who interfere with privacy.

'If protection is obtained, however, something of the utmost value is lost, viz: Nature's spaciousness and bounteousness in the matter of light and air.

Man cannot live naturally, that is healthily, if he is deprived of space, air and light.'

Once readers have overcome their astonishment that the good doctor can rabbit on at such length without mentioning sheds once, they may see that said rabbiting is, in fact, a virtual manifesto for Sheddism.

I'm a Mini Celebrity. Get Me In There

Look at this incomplete list of characteristics and achievements.

- Well-known voice on Scottish radio.
- Desk sergeant in *Taggart*.
- Wears ridiculous suits.
- Raises huge sums of money for charity with duck races.
- Met HM Queen in recognition of his contribution to broadcasting.
- Host of anarchic TV chat show.
- Sidekick of Miss Suzy Wang Bang.
- Reasonably masterful in all the building trades.
- Big mate of Dot Cotton from *Eastenders*.

We could go on. Allow us to introduce John Manning, Mini Celebrity (as he calls himself), creator and sole constructor of Dot's Dooket (what's a dooket? See below).

John's friend June Brown is the actress who plays Dot Cotton, the chain-smoking, bible-thumping original in the cast of *Eastenders*. In real life she's a smoker too, like John, and here lie the origins of the dooket in question. You can't have a drag in the pub any more, so to build his own bar with his own rules seemed like John's perfect answer, and he would dedicate it to his pal. Dot's Dooket ran off the tongue better than June's Dooket, so that was that sorted. All he had to do then was design and build it.

He decided on an octagonal shape, rather than a plain box, and a historical look, as if it had always been there. He scoured the yards, skips and building sites for recyclables. John began his working life as a doer-up of old properties, which was when he learned his building skills and where to look for stuff, such as the bowling club souvenirs found where the ancient clubhouse had been demolished.

The Dooket is entirely his own work, including the interior, which features organ, pulpit and pews as a nod to Dot Cotton's character, and Soames. He is the undead figure in the photograph, who says things like 'Welcome, guest, to my Master's dooket,' or, indeed, anything John wants him to say.

Anticlockwise from below: Soames, June, John, and can't remember.

As well as that rare thing, a smokers' bar, the Dooket may also be classified as the smallest kirk in Scotland, and suitable arrangements could be made for any couple who want to get married in it.

Interesting, and it's a shed

Dooket or dookit is a Scots contraction of dovecote, and the word kept that meaning so long as dovecotes, or dookets, were commonplace. When Sir Walter Scott published *Guy Mannering* in 1815, readers were pleased to learn that moor-fowl were plentiful on Dandy Dinmont's farm; they lay 'as thick as doos in a dooket'.

Another Scottish novelist, John Galt, wrote in *The Entail*: 'Gang into the desk-head, and ye'll fin' a bonny sewt pocket-book in the doocot hole next the window'. 'Sewt' will be short for sewit, i.e. sewn or embroidered, but already we can see that the dovecot is changing from avian shelter to hidey-hole in general. The wee dookit by the fireplace can be just the sort of place where you used to keep your pipe and tobacco, while the dooket in John Manning's garden can be the place where you put that in your pipe and smoke it.

The Dooket is also the name of the par three seventh at Uphall Golf Club, West Lothian.

Steve's Oestrogen Retreat

Let us state here and now that female reproductive hormones do not make a subject on which we wish to dwell. When his wife Jenni calls Steve's shed his Oestrogen Retreat, she means no more than a refuge from those lady persons, such as spouse, daughters *et cetera*, who comprise his family and may sometimes wish him out of the way, or *vice versa*, and nothing to do with all that other stuff.

Steve says he didn't want the standard Australian galvanized iron shed with a concrete base and, looking at the pictures, we can certainly agree that he hasn't got that. He wanted a shed with a more of a vernacular feel, more rustic, like some of the huts in the Snowy Mountains.

The Snowies, for non Australians, are famous for being the highest and snowiest and so on, but are also the natural home of the bogong moth. This

Shipwright Jim, 92, and Steve in a calmer place.

moth, once the central delicacy of aboriginal feasting in high summer, is now better known as a terrible nuisance when it invades office blocks in Sydney and Canberra.

Roast moth notwithstanding, Steve searched for second-hand bits and pieces to give that sort of ockerish feel to his shed. He found stone from two old barns, stringybark wood from a wool shearing shed and jarrah floor joists from demolished houses.

There are well over 700 species of eucalyptus tree, most of them Australian natives including, you will hardly be surprised to learn, *Eucalyptus microtheca*, being the one beneath the shade of which the jolly swagman sat, *E. marginata*, the jarrah tree, and all thirty of the stringybarks. Two that grow together in the Adelaide hills are *E. baxteri*, the brown stringybark, and *E. oblique*, the messmate stringybark, and Steve's shed lining he thinks is probably a mixture of these.

To be even more reminiscent of old Australian buildings, Steve collected some of the narrow profile corrugated sheet they call mini orb iron, for the gable ends and low on the side walls, and a plan was devised in partnership with Steve's mate Jim, an 87-year-old ex shipwright. By the time the shed,

known as Jim's Hut in honour of his making the main frame and much else, reached the stage in the photograph, Jim was 92.

But why, you ask, does it need to be so big? Well, it has several purposes. The first is to house Steve's collections of bygones, of scales and balances, antique tools, ancient Japanese maps, furniture and other priceless relics of times past, which previously had filled the dining room at home and caused intra-family discussions.

There also had to be space for drinking beer and telling tales around the old pot-bellied stove, so that was the ground floor occupied. Above is the loft, empty at the time of writing, but destined to be 'a calmer place than the bottom room', as Steve puts it. Eventually it will have a bed and a comfortable sofa from which Steve, at his ease, can stare over his neighbour's grapevines.

Daughters Holly and Caitlin are eyeing the loft space for their own uses. Since the shed has been called The Oestrogen Retreat by Jenni, such uses are clearly out of the question.

The Cares that Infest the Day
Shall Fold their Tents, like the
Arabs, and as Silently Steal Away

H ere we have yet another example of poetry getting it wrong. The poet, Henry Wadsworth Longfellow (1807–1882) should have been expressing the notion that the cares infesting the day will unfold and steal away once you're in your shed or, in this case, tent, yurt, or gertee.

We have elsewhere in this book stated unequivocally that sheds are not domiciles. Residence in the shed disqualifies it from the definition. The exception that proves the rule is here included because it need not be lived in, and it could be the cheapest, most easily built, most personal green/sustainable tent-shed and, in its own way, it is a thing of beauty.

Is it a small Alaskan circus? No, it's two gertees.

Niki Raapana first came to Alaska in 1974, selling magazines door-to-door. In Fairbanks and Anchorage she worked as an entertainer, bartender and waiter, before moving into her true metier as writer and, later, website designer for, among others, Camp Redington, where she now lives. Tim Redington built the first full-size gertee frame to repay Niki for all her help, which she converted into a winter home.

Niki is now settled in her gertee as independent researcher, author and publisher who campaigns for natural rights to existence and all the forms that necessarily takes. To deny people the right to live off their natural resources, she says, is to deny them natural life. Once she realised that she can build herself a little hut wherever she goes, with whatever is there, the word 'freedom' took on a whole new meaning.

Camp Redington is part of a community called Kenny Lake, which is what the USA calls a Census Designated Place, that is to say it is a place because people live thereabouts, not because it has a town hall and a butter cross. Kenny Lake residents describe their CDP as 'rural Alaska', which says it all really. It's near an earlier settlement, Copper Center, another CDP, which actually began as a couple of tents in 1898, one grandly designated 'Hotel Holman' by its owner, Andrew Holman, to provide sustenance, shelter and postal services to prospectors on their way to and from the Klondike.

It's a fairly adventurous region, surrounded by high mountains, forests where the wild things are, and rivers that start off as glaciers, and roughly 160 miles in a straight line from Anchorage.

Niki Raapana: 'Here I am starting to camp for my fourth year in Kenny Lake, and it's been a trip to think about what changes have happened to my life since that first winter here in my trusty Girl Scout wall tent. I spent months freezing my ass off in that tent, wishing at least once every day that I had a yurt. I dreamed of owning a portable tent I could insulate well enough to hold some heat.'

And the dream came true, and it was called Gertee. 'Ger' is the Mongolian word (гэр – ghair); 'yurt' is Russian (юрта – yoorta). Gertees are standard yurts made from cheap, free and/or salvaged materials. Unlike the Mongolian version, with its ornate supporting woodwork and thick felt lined with gorgeous fabrics, representing the nomadic family wealth and the centre of the universe, the gertee is the budget variety. It can be made from rubbish and near-rubbish.

The basic plan is a circular wall made of lattice work, looking like the criss-cross panels you buy from the garden centre up which to grow your climbers (see King of the Wild Frontier, below). From the top of the wall, extending upwards is a conical arrangement of poles tied together at the top. Cover it all with whatever, and there you have your yurt-shed, or gertee. Of course, if you intend to overwinter in it, in Mongolia or Alaska for instance, the whatever needs to include some insulating material.

A sixteen-foot wide gertee needs about eighty wall slats. Individually they don't have to be very substantial but should make a wall five feet high or more. You could use metal strips or plastic pipes, tree branches, bamboo – anything you can tie together to make a lattice. If each slat meets other slats four times, that's 320 ties. Again, you can make the ties from anything that will do the job. Once tied together, the walls may concertina together and roll up should the nomadic urge strike you.

Now, roof poles. Eight is the minimum, nine feet long and at least two inches square or the equivalent round. The roof tie can be a ring, a square, or possibly not there at all if you choose to follow a tepee arrangement. The roof ring Niki settled on is a wooden octagon two feet across, under the roofing cover rather than open to let the smoke out.

Your gertee needs a door; make one or find one. The roof cover can be anything waterproof. Niki has used tent groundsheets, bits of tarpaulin and builder's plastic, fixed with weatherproof glue. Outside, the walls can be covered in pieces of fabric or the same kind of stuff used for the roof. Inside, fabrics are good, on top of a layer of foil insulation. Fit a stove and there you are. On warmth, we have Niki's own word for it: 'As for staying warm in a gertee … well, I'm in one right now (24th January, Alaska). It's a brisk forty below zero outside and I'm sitting at my desk in a thin sleeveless dress, wool socks and my slippers.'

Niki is bringing out a book about building gertees. Meanwhile, see www.nord.twu.net/acl, and/or www.nikiraapana.com.

TRUE OR FALSE?

The Great Pyramid of Dung
A Mongol village consists of a small collection of yurts, each of which can be dismantled in about half an hour. Usually there is some sort of corral to protect the weaker animals from wolves, although huge, shaggy and very fierce dogs effectually keep off marauders. They are also the scavengers, eating the bodies of any animals that die. Sheep are kept near the village; they are looked after by the children. Their droppings (the sheep's, not the children's) are valuable; an important feature of every village is the great pyramid of dried dung which, in this treeless country, takes the place of wood for burning.

For. I. Am a Pirate King, Hurrah, Hurrah for our Pirate King. And it is, it is, a Glorious Thing, to be a Pirate King

Thus spake W.S. Gilbert and Sir Arthur Sullivan, recognising that such a personage must have a fine poop cabin (at the blunt end, from the Latin *puppis*, the stern of a ship) filled with spoils and treasure, and a parrot. The parrot in this case is not called Captain Flint, after Long John Silver's, but Duffy, he being in the family for thirty years and so dating from long before Pirate King Reg Miller's pirate thing.

Although born on Romford market and a lifelong trader from insecure premises, Reg only converted relatively recently to saltwater thievery, wild roving in quest of plunder and depredation upon navigable rivers. However, he has always been unable to resist the acquisition of odd objects and unconsidered trifles, or 'collecting' as people call it. Favoured items included knives, Buddhas, blunderbusses and anything to do with rum.

Who's a pretty boy, then? That's Reg with the glasses.

Display of these seemed to suit the old house he used to live in, but they didn't look right in the new place he moved to, so the whole lot went in the loft for ten years.

Then came his moment, at the cinema of all places, when a scene set on a pirate ship brought involuntary words to his lips: 'I want one of them'. Apart from a family shed-raising in the early stages, and some help with digging out the Caribbean dock, or fish pond, it has been Reg's project, entirely constructed from recycled and reclaimed materials, including the panelled doors rescued from skips. Dimensions are sixteen feet wide by eight feet deep and ten feet six at the apex.

In the words of the King himself: 'The inside of the shed is fully equipped with a dead man's chest, and outside there is plenty of space for roistering and carousing among the tropical plants and under the palm thatched lean-to. The front of the shed opens completely to make the most of the evening sun and provides a suitable location for card playing, rum drinking and bad behaviour of every kind.'

See www.readersheds.co.uk Shed of the Year Winner, 2010, *The Lady Sarah out of Worthing.*

Interesting, and it's in the shed

The crossed bones are real but this ram's skull with marbles for eyes is a replica. After several rums, it seems real enough.

Sarah, schoolteacher and queen consort to HM Reg, is a total supporter of the shed – which is named after her – and uses it, with her computer, as an office when preparing her lessons. So we think this photograph is a put-up job.

King of the Wild Frontier

THIS SMALL yurt under construction is a special travelling model, being built by a rather remarkable man called Tim Redington. The roof ring is his design, made out of a dustbin lid and welded with steel pipe inserts. The roof poles are five-foot PVC pipe and the five-foot PVC walls are riveted.

Tim was born in the Territory of Alaska in 1949, when Anchorage was still a tent city. His childhood was spent on several family homesteads and mining claims. While many Alaskans anxiously pursued modernity, the Redingtons were making a dog-sled journey, backward in time.

The nine-year-old Tim could stay alone in the Alaskan wilderness, feeding and caring for 250 dogs. He learned to trap and shoot and skin and prepare his

own meat. He and his brothers pretty much hunted and trapped all winter and fished, gardened and preserved food all summer. He describes his early life as 'living more like Indians than the Indians'.

Uneducated in city ways, or even village ways, Tim's life today is not so different, which is why he needs his collapsible, transportable gertee, as a base for his winter's hunting and trapping. The pictures show the construction. Those among us who do not have the opportunity to spend seasons in nomadic style may still consider this format as a model for our next shed, don't you think?

See www.campredington.com.

Art in the Shed

G one are the days when the least attentive person would know when he or she was in an artist's studio. Looking around, one would see paint, brushes, canvas, nude models, charcoal and empty beer crates. That has mostly disappeared because the artist's traditional survival strategy, the talent for depiction, has become less relevant to the ecosystem.

As with so many other endangered animals, the cause of the trouble lies in a complete failure to adapt to changing circumstances. The traditional artist, retreating into a shed from an expensive studio with north-facing windows, will continue to attempt to emulate or surpass previous artistic achievements. This is futile. The new breed, the Conceptual, or Con, Artist has realised that there is no point in trying to paint something better than – say – The Odalisque, when you can video a naked woman sitting on the toilet. This is a doubly effective strategy because, when people get tired of looking at the woman on the bog, they can record an episode of *The Simpsons* over the top of it.

Con Artists may have no visible signs of talent, for depiction or anything else, but they can easily persuade a squillionaire or a local council to give a huge grant so that a room can be filled with chicken noodle soup.

The conventional and much less assertive normal artist, trying to find some cash for paint to do a picture of Exmoor at sunset, has no recourse to wealthy sponsors who, as they would, want something new. Loads and loads of artists have already painted landscapes, and thousands and thousands and millions of people have such pictures hanging in rooms which, more creatively, could be filled with soup.

So, a call goes out to shed-based artists everywhere. Follow the example of Miss Moony Lampstandard, of Wahpeton, Dickinson County, Iowa, who bought a large mirror, took it to her shed, painted it over with some whitewash she had there, and called the work 'Where are you?' At an exhibition held in the main library of the nearby University of Okoboji, Miss Lampstandard was delighted to attach the red 'Sold' dot to her art and to bank a cheque sufficient to pay for four round-the-world cruises and to buy a ninety-nine year lease on a massive studio with north-facing windows.

She told the *Dickinson County News*: 'It is vitally important that people should not be restricted by an artist's work. They should be able to give imagination free rein and not be forced down particular visual avenues by, for instance, a picture of a horse.'

Miss Lampstandard's next great *oeuvre*, a blank sheet of hardboard eight feet by four, framed in white plastic beading, will be called 'Ideas waiting to occur' as soon as she's back from her fourth world cruise.

It was while she was on her third that the brilliant notion of 'Marsupialness' hit her like a slap from a wet haddock. Full of enthusiasm, she rounded up ten of the beefiest crewmen and dressed them in Armani sunglasses, hand-knitted hairnets of bright blue nylon sea-fishing line, and very loose-fitting Harris Tweed plus-fours. The left legs of these trousers were filled variously and severally with custard powder, easycook rice, caraway seeds and, begged from the on-ship boutique, some of those bits of polystyrene packaging that fly all over the place.

Cruising folk were invited to feel inside the trousers and transfer the contents of a left leg into a right leg, having first bought a ticket and waited in an orderly queue.

TRUE OR FALSE?

A Gnome in the Shed

… is worth two by the pond. This and other well known phrases and sayings, proverbial maxims and sage saws, often of an obscure nature though generally meant to guide the unwary through life's trials, are actually called 'gnomes'. Originally, gnomes were a Greek thing and were strung together in verses by poets of the sixth century BC such as Theognis, Phocylides and Gnomonides. An example might be: 'Keep your onions in your shed, and finish off your leeks instead'. Luckily, very little of their work survives but they can be credited with starting the trains of thought that eventually led to moral philosophy.

More importantly for us, the ancient gnomic traditions were upheld in Anglo-Saxon, and the Anglo-Saxon Gnomic Verses, pagan poetic riddles, prove that Sheddism is as old – and, indeed, gnomic – as civilisation itself.

University scholars over the centuries have been unable to explain the real messages behind these verses, because they have been approaching the problem in the wrong way, which in turn is because there are too few sheds in the groves of academe. We have already seen the close association between

Anglo-Saxons and sheds, so this gives us the clue about what we need to do. We need to look at these verses from a sheddish point of view.

To quote: *Sceomiande man sceal in sceade hweorfan, scir in leohte geriseð* .

The key words in this gnomic sentence are *sceomian* – shame, *scir* – sheer, clear, transparent, and *leohte* – light. The literal translation is something like: The shamed man shall wander in the shade, (but) it is fitting that the transparent man (shall walk) in the light.

Gnomic verses were not written to be literal. The meaning here is much more poetic: 'It's a shame for the rest of you people, but only from inside a shed can the light be clearly seen.'

Woodman, Spare That Tree!
Touch Not a Single Bough!
In Youth it Sheltered Me,
And I'll Protect it Now

Whether or not Roger Darbshire was inspired by the deathless poesy of George Pope Morris, so memorably set to music by Henry Russell in 1837, the result is the same. A eucalyptus, one of the hardy versions that will stand a winter in Moreton-in-the-Marsh, grew tall in

Roger's small front garden. There was no back garden, and no room around the house to build the extension the family demanded, but Roger would not cut down his gum tree.

A scheme for a shed would have to be devised, incorporating the arborial inconvenience within. Roger could see the problem. Trees sway in the breeze. They grow. In fact, gum trees have an advanced reputation in both respects. His cunning plan was for a shroud around the tree where it would pierce the roof, being one layer of old truck tyre inner-tube, with a second layer of roofing felt in an overlapping fan. In the event, the felt proved not to be a total success, lacking the necessary flexibility, so a more sophisticated answer in oiled leather, a hand-made 'boot', was planned to be sewn in place and, to attack from the other angle, the tree would be lopped to half its size to reduce swaying.

But we get ahead of ourselves. First, there was the pile of oak at the wood yard, sliced four inches thick and ten feet by two feet, each board about three hundredweight, but only twenty quid a board as opposed to the normal ten times that. Thus was the frame decided. Weatherboarding on the front is mostly elm plus some ash, an inch thick, and the back and sides are pine.

Roger is a keen carpentry hobbyist so he knows about wood. His wavy roof is Canadian western red cedar shingles, window frames are variously oak, yew and ash, inside flooring is keruang, a red tropical plantation hardwood (going

Roger's house will fall down before his shed does.

very cheap to offset the eco-guilt – come on, we've all done it). He bought the elm front door from a reclamation yard and put the window in himself.

In the manner of a Luton van, there's an additional sleeping platform or storage space (or space for storing a sleeper), some eight feet by six, suspended three feet below the roof and supported from beneath by a peeled ash trunk. This is called The Mezzanine, which is one of those many words we bandy about without really knowing what they mean. In this case, there isn't much to know. *Mezzanino* is Italian for small middle or lesser middle.

Bandy is more interesting, probably coming from an old French verb no longer in common use, *bander*, to bandie, describing the act of whacking the ball back and forth in tennis (real tennis, naturally, not your modern lawn variety). Anyone doubting that is referred to *The Duchess of Malfi*, the blood and guts drama by Shakespearean near-contemporary John Webster, in which Bosola says 'We are merely the stars' tennis-balls, struck and bandied which way please them'. It doesn't quite have the ring of King Lear's lines 'As flies to wanton boys, are we to the gods; they kill us for their sport', but that only goes to show why we say 'Brush up your Shakespeare' more often than we say 'Brush up your Webster'.

Just to show there is no end to the erudition of the shed, it struck Roger that his ash trunk was like Yggdrasil, the great Tree of the World in Norse mythology, said to be an ash. This is not the sort of thought that would strike everybody. We must therefore hope, for the sake of the mezzanine, that Niðhöggr (say nith-herger) the malicious dragon is not gnawing at the roots, as he is wont to do.

A tale of two trees. The gum tree grows behind the chair (previous page) while the bare ash trunk supports the mezzanine, reached by home-made ladder.

TRUE OR FALSE?

New Sheddism Eliminates Housewives

Not very long ago, when the shed was almost exclusively the dominion of the male, the female of the species could often be described, by herself and others, as a Housewife. Now, as every last bastion of every male enclave has become common ground, and whether or not the decline of the Housewife is an equal and opposite reaction to the female investment of shed territory, we have to wonder where are they who, in bygone days, would have become Housewives. Are they in the shed?

A bastion, incidentally, we are intrigued to learn, is a projecting earthwork fortification in the shape of an irregular pentagon, so what that has to do with it, goodness only knows.

There used to be a great many books written about the habitat and seasonal behaviour of Housewife, for instance *Every Woman's Book of Home Making* published in the 1930s which states: 'A large proportion of the Housewife's time is occupied in planning, buying and preparing food, and indeed this is one

of her biggest responsibilities. If, through lack of knowledge, the Housewife does not provide body-building foods, then the children will be rickety and stunted.' It also says 'Many people spend too much money on jam, sugar and sweets', so some things don't change – but some do.

'Monday. The Front Bedroom. If you do not intend washing the blankets, hang them out on a clean line in the sunshine to air thoroughly.'

'Friday. The Living Room. Take up carpets and rugs, place heavy furniture in centre of room and cover with dust sheets. Clean ceiling and walls and wash all paintwork. Wash all china, glass and other ornaments. Beat all rugs and mats out in the open.'

The list of essential household cleaning equipment has fifty-two items, from Double banister brush, Small single banister brush, Self-wringing mop, Wire mattress brush and Zinc and enamelled pails, to Powdered Whiting.

Maybe there is scope here for a collection of bygones in the shed, but anybody asking for Powdered Whiting in the fishmonger's will be disappointed.

No such books are written now except to present aspects of Housewife's activities as pastimes, leisure crafts, ways to self-empowerment or, in acute cases, the new rock and roll. Cookery books are especially popular although many of their purchasers rarely cook anything except perhaps at weekends. These people, we are sure, do not have a shed. Instead, they have kitchens with the finest professional equipment in battleship-quality stainless steel. They have built-in satellite microwaves that can play DVDs of Jamie Oliver, fridges that automatically order the semi-skimmed from Harrods, Art Nouveau chandeliers and dangling bunches of herbs.

Confronted with the latest celebrity-chef dinner party fancy with its obscure international ingredients and its every element stated to the hundredth of a gram, someone may spend all Saturday trying to make it. While doing so, she/he will imagine four or five beautiful people around her/him, quaffing wine while helping to remove the outside leaves from the zamponi and scoring the krupuk with a sharp knife.

Housewife as was, Lady Sheddie as is, confronted by said fancy recipe, will pick up the idea, turn it around, substitute what's available for what isn't and produce something practical from among all the nonsense.

Take 'Oyster Relish' from *A Plain Cookery Book for the Working Classes* by Charles Elme Francatelli, once Chief Cook to Queen Victoria. This little book was published in 1852 but it still made perfect sense in 1952 and, to some we are sure, perfect sense now:

> 'Put the oysters, with their liquor and a little water or milk, into a saucepan; add a bit of butter kneaded, that is, well mixed with a table-spoonful of flour; pepper and a little salt; stir the oysters over the fire until they have gently boiled for about five minutes, and then pour them into a dish containing some slices of toasted bread. Strew all over their surface equal quantities of bread raspings and grated cheese; hold a red-hot shovel over the top until it becomes slightly coloured and eat this little delicacy hot.'

Here's the test. Are you asking yourself questions, such as: a bit of butter – how much is a bit? How many oysters? How many bread raspings? What's a rasping? Have we got a shovel, darling? When the red-hot shovel becomes slightly coloured, what colour should it be?

Or have you already worked out your own way of doing it?

This wondrous shed with nailed-up tidy-jars belongs to Hull photographer Kostas Bozikis.
He says it is a mess. See www.bozikis.co.uk

The Dangers of Over-Shedding

The traditional doctrines and hallowed girders of shed structuralism are crumbling everywhere. Wives, partners and live-in girlfriends, according to folklore, have always been glad to see the men in their lives disappearing out of the back door and heading for the shed, but here we have an instance of Madame making it plain that shed-time must be curtailed.

Initially, there was no problem. Roger Taylor of Elenham, Essex, always had a shed but he decided to build the shed to end sheds, a monster of 288 square feet, to house his model railway with additional space for refrigerator, television, armchair and other necessities of life. Entirely by himself, he took a year over it, a huge effort and, naturally, once such a project was complete, he had to make full use of it. He called it 'Allambi', which is an Australian aboriginal word that he learned as a boy, son of parents who were ten-pound Poms, meaning 'a quiet place'. That was the idea. Retreat, dog house, haven, allambi, call it what you will, the purpose was manifest.

Roger was a train driver. He used to drive the Norwich intercity out of Stratford, often the newspaper train on the journey out and the normal passenger service back at around 7am, which means he must have conveyed your correspondent who often caught that very train from Diss in those days. You could get a soft-boiled egg and toast in the buffet car.

Real railways have termini, beginnings and ends, whereas model railways have no end. Your creation is never complete and, should your significant other detest model railways, well, this can lead to upsets.

And so it came to pass that the railway was sold, the fridge and TV removed, and a certain amount of household junk allowed in. Roger still goes in his shed, but not as much. There he makes railway signs, perfect replicas in wood of the old metal ones, which he sells. 'Penalty for trespassing, forty shillings. LNER.'

Interesting, and it was in the shed

Those who do not enthuse over model railways, for example Mrs Taylor of Essex, can point in their bewilderment to the entry in a pre-war edition of *Encyclopaedia Britannica*, which lists the proper uses of models. First,

they are for educational purposes. Second, they are for exhibitions and publicity. 'Last, but not least, there is the use of models for the instruction and amusement of the young, in the form of model railways, model power boats, sailing yachts and other high-class toys'.

The writer, one Wenman Joseph Bassett-Lowke, goes on to state that 'Model-making is a hobby almost peculiar'. To be fair, we should complete the sentence – 'to the British Isles and has many enthusiastic adherents'. Rather than 'British Isles' we can be sure, if he had been writing today in the post-Imperial global village, he might have put 'the English speaking world, just as it is with sheds'.

Bassett-Lowke is a name well known among railway modellers, through the firm W.J. founded soon after his twenty-first birthday, which was 27 December 1898. His company is now subsumed into Corgi/Hornby. The Bassett-Lowke Society meets once a quarter at the Red Lion Hotel, Hatfield, when, doubtless, one will not be able to turn around without bumping into someone who has a shed.

By 'other high-class toys', Bassett-Lowke was indubitably thinking of Meccano. However, the original patent for Meccano did not mention the name. It said:

'Hornby's Improved Toy or Educational Device for Children and Young People relates to arrangements by which children can construct mechanical objects, buildings etc from independent pieces. The equipment may include a file, screwdriver and pliers for working the pieces. The pieces serve for the construction of bridges, tunnels, stations, signals, signal boxes, hoists and buildings in general, as well as cranes and railway lines.'

FEMALES' CHEAP TRIP,

FROM

PRESTON TO FLEETWOOD.

THE Committee who managed the Poor People's Trip to Fleetwood have arranged for

ANOTHER TRIP

to the same place on MONDAY, August 6th, to start from Maudland Station at half-past Eight in the morning, and return from Fleetwood, at Seven in the evening.

Female's Tickets, and Schools, and Children under 12 years of age, there and back .... 0s. 9d.

Men's ditto ... . 1s. 6d.

To be had of Mr. G. CARTWRIGHT, Fishergate; Mr. J. DEARDEN, Butler's Court; Mr. J. HARGREAVES, London-road; Mr. R. WALSH, 64, Brunswick-street, and at the *Guardian* Office.

The arrangements will afford an opportunity to a vast number of females who were anxious to purchase tickets for the last trip, but being a charity one could not be allowed. Employers, also, who do not arrange for trips on their own account, may avail themselves of this opportunity of sending down any of the sick or other hands whom they may be desirous of treating. A steamer will ply through the day to take persons round the Light-house at 2d. each. Arrangements are also made for Bathing in the Victoria Baths at a low charge; and (weather permitting) for other out-door amusements.

ADVICE.

Be at the station, at least, ten minutes before the hour announced for departure, and take your seats in the carriages without delay. If you have friends they will find you much more readily in the carriages than in a crowd. Have your tickets ready to show as you enter the station. Be careful to put your ticket in a place of safety during your stay in Fleetwood, as in case of loss, you will be obliged to pay your fare back. Above all things show an accommodating disposition, and a wish to oblige; this will materially assist in making the excursion pleasant. Do not attempt to leave your seats till the train is fully stopped at Fleetwood. Do not Bathe too near the public promenades. The Bathing Machines are stationed at the North Beach, terms, 6d. each.

Interesting, but it's not a shed

In 1849, long before there was any thought of 'females' being in the shed – or, indeed, of anyone, male or female, having a model railway – said females could travel half price from Preston for a day at the seaside. Of course, and above all things, they had to show an accommodating disposition and a wish to oblige, thus materially assisting in making the excursion pleasant.

Based solely on the retail price index, one shilling and sixpence (eighteen pence) in 1849 would represent about £6 today, so half-price females were paying three quid for their fares and two quid for the bathing machine plus, we would guess, another two quid for lunch. As well as the RPI, if we take into account what a mill girl would be earning at that time, versus modern wages, that will give us a closer estimate of affordability rather than just price. Now we're talking £25 for the half-price fare on the amazing novelty steam railway, fifty quid for the boyfriend, plus fish and chips, beer, tea and cake later…it soon mounts up, as mother used to say.

TRUE OR FALSE?

Your Hour upon the Stage

Have you noticed how, the older you get, the faster time seems to fly? So, the less time left in your life, the less and less you want to waste any of it. If you are going to fritter your time away jogging, or worrying about the amount of salt and transfats there might be in a cocktail sausage, do it while you are young and time moves more slowly. Then, when you're older, you can slow time down by being in your shed.

On the other hand, you are only young once.

Monet in the Signal Box

When they closed the LNER freight line between Castle Eden Colliery in County Durham and Stockton-on-Tees, it wasn't bad news for everyone. For example, it meant that groups of small boys could play along the line and harmlessly enter the signal boxes and pull all the levers. When the men came to take up the track, the boys could sometimes hitch a ride on some of the last steam locos in England. Happy days.

For most of those lads, it was no more than a lark. For Paul Kingston, it was one of those imprinting experiences that would, eventually, lead to a rather fine shed in Dumfries and Galloway. It was the buildings he was attracted to, the old stations and so on. He says 'I have always liked signal boxes', and that's a sentiment that many will share. Signal boxes do have a certain something about them.

So, when he decided to have a shed, he looked around and saw how much money a new one would be. That led him to consider building one, and then

The only signal box with a carpet.

came a flash of inspiration. If he was going to do it himself, he might as well do it in style.

He researched designs and found that signal boxes had no standard pattern, so he picked one individual, made a drawing, and set about it, mainly as a summerhouse for his wife Karen (known as Kat – 'she likes railways') and daughter Amy. Karen was providing the budget; Paul was building it for her, in his spare time from his work as a gardener. Glass for windows came from eBay, as did the Victorian lock, the door came out of a skip, and the stove would have a genuine guard's van flue pipe. The paint was good old British Railways cream and maroon, and the sign was Thorpe Thewles, Paul's home village.

A subsidiary use would be as a studio for Paul, who is a great admirer of Monet and paints skyscapes, clouds and sunsets, after the manner of the master. He keeps his paints in a toolbox, which is what attracted some local scallywags who tried to break in. Finding the Victorian lock too much for them, they smashed a window and tried to prise the roof off but never did find out that there were no tools in the toolbox. Only paints.

TRUE OR FALSE?

A Dead Mouse

John Mayow, (1640–1679), Fellow of All Souls' College, Oxford, was a man ahead of his time. A good century before Priestley and Lavoisier made their discoveries about oxygen, he deduced that one fourteenth part of air consisted of a substance necessary to the life of small rodents. He showed this by going into his shed, where he kept some pet mice. He placed one of them, called Ferdy, in a jar inverted over water. Ferdy used up the said substance and died when the jar was approximately one fourteenth full of water.

You can repeat this experiment and get a similar result but you, unlike Mayow, will know that the constituents of the gas breathed out by mammals are not the same as those breathed in. The fourteenth fraction was a false answer, oxygen being about a fifth of air, but was understandable when the experimenter did not take account of Ferdy's exhalations.

Further, Mayow did not draw the obvious conclusion, of mice and men needing something in the air. He was blind to this at least partly because it was believed that the human body was inhabited by an independent spirit, or soul, which governed the life-sustaining functions. When the spirit departed, breathing stopped through lack of management; physical factors were not involved.

Robert Hooke, (1635–1703), later showed that a dog with no ribs or diaphragm could be kept alive with bellows, and therefore that it was not the act of breathing, regulated by unseen forces, that was vital, but the air itself and what, mysteriously, was in it.

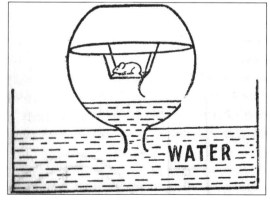

No expense has been spared in commissioning the most accomplished artists to produce diagrams for this book. As you can see, a mouse with quite a long tail and big ears is crouching on a kind of diving platform but is unwilling to jump in. This is all part of the plan.

If You Go Down in the Woods Today

In Cornwall, anyway, you might not see so many bears but you may be lucky enough to espy, creeping cryptically through the undergrowth, The Ivy Man. Not to be confused with The Green Man or, indeed, the milkman, the venerable Ralph Thurston will be seeking inspiration which, for him, consists in very particular formations of ivy growing around fallen trees.

We can do no better at this juncture than to quote the poet Percy Bysshe Shelley, (1792–1822) who, in his short life, wrote quite a lot of what in Norfolk is called 'squit' but also managed the occasional shining gem, as thus from *Prometheus Unbound*:

'He will watch from dawn to gloom
The lake-reflected sun illume
The yellow bees in the ivy-bloom,
Nor heed, nor see, what things they be;
But from these create he can
Forms more real than living man,
Nurslings of immortality.'

When he finds his prize, an entanglement of ancient ivy around an even more ancient trunk, Ralph sees – not what the rest of us might, such as a bit of old ivy on a rotten old tree – but a form more real than living man, a work of natural art which, like all such, is immortality in miniature.

In his shed, Ralph gradually cuts away all the stuff that is not art, perhaps murmuring to himself the lines from *The Graham Tartan to a Graham* by Louise Imogen Guiney (1861–1920): 'Use me in honour; cherish me, as ivy

from a sacred tree'. His objective is a fantastical dancing, writhing, entwining form as you can see in the picture. He calls the process 'whittling', and the raw material for his creation 'wood', and such modest, plain terms could well be adopted with advantage by those who seek the Turner Prize with work more difficult to appreciate than Ralph's.

His shed, incidentally, came with the property and had a name: The Herring House. From this we may imagine salt fish, oak chippings, smoke, and thick tar on the walls as we find in the kippering shed of Messrs Fortune of Whitby (established 1872), but no. Not a sign of it. So that's something of a perplexity but never mind. Ralph, safe from passive kipper smoking, can carry on whittling.

> Oh roses for the flush of youth,
> And laurel for the perfect prime;
> But pluck an ivy branch for me
> Grown old before my time.
>
> *Christina Rossetti (1830–1894)*

TRUE OR FALSE?

Pets in the Shed

Should you want to keep a wild animal in your shed, you need to know how to catch it, because every kind of beast has to be captured in its own special way. Polar bears, for example, are usually lassoed by hunters in canoes, so you need some mates to go with you unless, of course, you are already on good terms with people who live in the Arctic.

The standard method is with three or four canoes tied together. As soon as the bear is roped, it swims away as hard as it can, dragging the canoes behind, until it is exhausted. You and your colleagues then get your paddles out, or possibly start your outboard motors, and tow your bear to a safe haven where it will be too tired to resist being put in a cage.

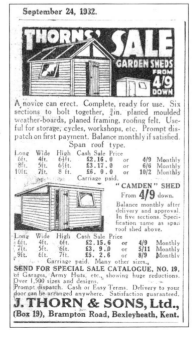

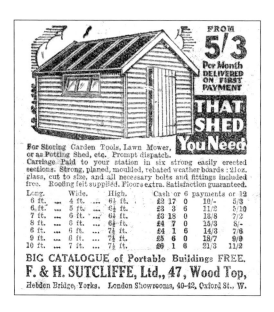

Giraffes are normally hunted on horseback with lassoes. Fully-grown giraffes, which are eighteen feet high, will not go under railway and other bridges without bashing their heads. They cannot be trained to duck and so, unless the way to your shed is clear of such obstacles, it is best to catch the younger and smaller ones. Nevertheless, the eventual height of your new pet must be an influence in the matter of shed design.

Ostriches are taken the same way as giraffes but the difference lies in the animal itself. An ostrich is the village idiot of the plains; once caught, it is only necessary to put a sock over its head and it can be led anywhere. You and a friend can then hold a wing each to guide the bird to its destination. The type of sock is important. It should be large, stretchy and made of good wool. The ostrich must not be able to see through it, otherwise it will kick you very hard indeed in your private parts.

Mountain goats and wild Soay sheep present a problem because they are inclined to be nervous and may hurt themselves while struggling to escape. It is a good idea to build a sedan-chair-cum-cage, which is padded with local materials such as bracken and moss or something fluffy from the DIY store. Once the animal is in the padded cell, as it were, it can be carried down the mountain without too much difficulty.

A drawback with many undomesticated creatures is that they can become sulky in captivity and go off their food. Condensed milk has been found to be the best thing to restore their appetites.

What's a Shed? That's One, Over There

If we all thought we knew what a shed is, look at this. Botticelli meets Robert Adam meets Argos. In the words of Edward Lear – 'who, or why, or which, or what?'

For the answer, we must travel to a suburban garden in Exeter where Mr and Mrs Cooper decided to give a small shed each to their son and daughter

as their respective private domains. The boy Philip, aged only five, decided that his shed was the Rose Cottage Hotel, while his elder sister Elizabeth named hers Madame's Café. They set up a communications system – two World War One telephones and some wire – and opened for imaginary business.

Three years later, the boy was looking through an Argos catalogue and saw a chandelier for fourteen quid. Something went click in his brain and his life's destiny was settled. But first, he had to have that chandelier for his shed. He washed cars, hoovered the house, sold his toys, raised the money, and his parents bought him the chandelier for his birthday so he could spend his cash on other items of shed decor. By the time he was fourteen years old, he and his shed were a multi-page feature in no less a magazine than *The World of Interiors*.

He was on his way to becoming a top designer but he still showed admirable shed characteristics. The curtains were trimmed with pyjama cords. He did a lot of his own plasterwork but, where he had to, he bought niches from the builder's merchant, cherubs in the department store meant for Christmas decorations, Botticelli's Primavera from the poster shop, wall lights from the pound shop and, with all together in his mind as a scheme, produced a neoclassical extravaganza.

It's all in the blood, of course. Mother had a shed as a child and used to make tea in there on a methylated spirits stove. Father had a shed where he did his paintings, so maybe there's artistic talent in the family as well as sheddism.

Interesting, but it's not a shed

The design brief for Philip Cooper's seaside 'shed' (previous page) was to create an eye-stopper for the reception area of Venture Three (a London firm of brand consultants) out of lolly sticks, on a seaside theme, costing £500. He used chip forks as well.

Selfridge's rooftop garden used to be the scene of many glamorous events, so when Philip was asked to design a pop-up restaurant there, for chef Pierre Koffman (La Tante Claire, three Michelin stars), he wanted to reinvent the magic and give diners 'a slightly surreal experience'. Note the lighting in Gordon Selfridge's favoured hat, and the wrought-iron garden gate.

Philip, after all sorts of media followed up the magazine article, had visitors queuing outside, which interrupted his further improvements and routine maintenance. The shed got wet in the Devon winter and dried out in the summer, creating a cycle of rot and pest invasion that required a constant battle. Eventually, with Philip away at university, Devon won and the most precious remains of the shed now rest in the parents' attic.

Advice on Pottering

Helen Dillon is a famous gardener and writer of many books and magazine articles on the subject, and she has a wonderful garden you can visit (see www.dillongarden.com). As a professional, she uses her shed for purposes some of us might find rather esoteric, for example storing plants that need a dry winter such as *Rhodohypoxis*, or the bulbous plants that need a warm, dry rest period in summer, like *Ixia*, *Sparaxis*, *Lachenalia*, *Gladiolus tristis*, *Tecophilaea*, *Tropaeolum azureum* and so on but, for Helen, it's still a shed.

A shed should, she says, have two exits in case you need to escape from approaching visitors who have been undeterred by the banging noises you have been making with a trowel and a galvo watering can. And do not place your shed in a shady, hidden corner of the garden. Have a south-facing window, so you can watch the setting sun through the cobwebs.

Make sure it's big enough, which is twice as big as you think it will be. You will cover the floor with stuff (in Helen's case, buckets of different compost mixes which all look the same but are unlabelled) and fill the shelves with things you don't want to throw away such as pieces of copper tube, ceiling roses, broken sprayer parts, bags of fertiliser granules that have solidified into concrete, oyster shells, ancient runner bean seeds in a tobacco tin, and that pretty glass marble you found.

Each Christmas you will acquire two big tins, one that held sweets, and one that held chocolate biscuits. One day, you will sort out all the nails, screws, hinges and whatnot into these tins; meanwhile, your tin collection becomes quite impressive. There will be jam jars amain, washed ready for chutney and pickled onions, although you refuse to acknowledge the fact that you will never make fifty jars of chutney. There will be wine bottles, for when you make that wine you are going to make.

There may be a shelf holding almost-empty bottles and packets of all the garden aids that you can't get any more because, according to the elfin safety, if you swam in a bath of any effective pesticide for two years you would have a one percent chance of contracting cancer of the toenail. Commercial growers can get these products and use millions of bathfuls a year, but you can't get anything that will kill a caterpillar or a codling moth. We can only hope that, while you could, you bought enough winter tar wash and other such incorrect substances to last you a while.

The alternative, as Helen says, is to collect all slugs, place them tenderly on a lettuce leaf and drive them out to the country before setting them free. Also, you can squish individually between finger and thumb each whitefly that gets in your greenhouse or attacks your brassicas in swarms in a hot summer. While squishing whitefly on your sprouts, you should compliment the caterpillars on their skill in turning your plants into Honiton lace.

The question now arises as to whether one should have a potting shed, or a pottering shed. Pottering, according to the Shorter Oxford, is the act of occupying oneself in an ineffectual or trifling way. Potting is the act of drinking (of ale etc), the making of pottery, the preserving of butter, meat, fish etc in pots, and planting/transplanting into pots. So, we should say, you can have either or both.

Secrets of the Shed

The people in this book who do things in their sheds – other than those activities we might group together under 'leisure' – are generally following a particular skill they have discovered in themselves, or a long-held ambition. You, dear reader, may have neither the skill nor the ambition to make mad nesting boxes, collect pillar boxes, compose music, follow the teachings of B.K.S. Iyengar, pamper a bearded dragon, paint clouds or construct the ultimate model railway network. You may, indeed, be very happy not doing anything at all in your shed.

Even so, we believe that hidden abilities and unfelt desires lurk within many of the Shed Tendency. It is therefore our duty to offer an idea for something that pretty well anybody can do in the shed, but we cannot reveal the name of the shed-person from whom the idea is copied (with permission). You see, you are going to find out how to make a fake antique.

It's a tatty old stool in a tatty old photograph, but it's the real thing, and you'd have to pay in the high hundreds and more if you found it in an antique shop. Do be careful, though. It might have been made recently, by a person in a shed.

We are not really out to fool whatsisname on the Antiques Road Show, but we do expect to fool the next door neighbour and the man on the galloping horse.

For an example, let's take a seventeenth century board stool. In those early, pioneering times, techniques and tools were fairly primitive and ambitions consequently modest so, if we are to fake in the Jacobean style, we must have a do-it-for-fun, cavalier attitude rather than serious precision and furrowed brows. In making our brand new antique, it actually helps if we begin with joinery which is not perfectly straight, level, smooth and right-angled.

We are not making a direct copy. The photographs are there for guidance, but each fake piece is an individual article. It is not so much a clone as a close relation of something genuine.

Your Jacobeans couldn't go to the wood merchant and buy planed and sanded oak, cut for them in convenient widths and lengths. They didn't have an electric jigsaw or a power drill. You will also need a hammer and a few odds and ends but, compared to the men in leather aprons, you have it very easy.

We are not going to give precise dimensions, because they don't matter. You can see from the pictures that you have five pieces to cut, and that the height of the stool is about the same as the length of the top. The top would usually be between eighteen and twenty inches long, with grain longways, twelve to fourteen inches wide and ¾ inch thick.

Legs and sides can be ½ inch. Legs are about two inches narrower than the top, to give the overhang. Sides are about eight inches wide. Any decorative cuttings-out with your jigsaw must be kept simple. You could just drill a few large holes in a pattern.

The four pieces of the frame are joined by slots the thickness of the wood. To join eight inch sides to legs, that's four inches up from the bottom edge and four inches down from the top of the leg. The slots in the sides should be at an angle. If your side piece is eighteen inches long, the gap inside your legs at the top edge should be about twelve inches and at the bottom edge about thirteen-and-a-half inches.

The Jacobean maker would have used nothing more to hold the frame together, but then his stool was only going to be sat on. His stool wasn't going to be thrown around, soaked, shot at and otherwise attacked (see below). You shall use glue. Depending on the accuracy of your slot cutting, you may need to tie string around the leg pieces to keep them in order while the glue sets.

Now to fix the top. Drill holes (quarter-of-an-inch) through the top into the legs, one at each corner, and two more at the mid-point into the sides. Do this by eye. Do not measure.

Pegs were usually of willow, but pine will do. Make square section lengths like very fat match sticks, slightly thicker than the holes you have drilled. If your peg-wood has good straight grain you can split it with a chisel; otherwise saw it. Drop some glue in the hole and bang a peg in fearlessly with a hammer. Saw off surplus, not too close.

No matter how much you distress a piece of furniture, if you don't get the right colour and patina of age it will look like a distressed new piece of furniture. With oak, there is only one way to get that perfect, 500-year-old look, and that is to make your board stool and wait 500 years. Every other method is a compromise but some are extremely good compromises.

The expert looks for a texture to the wood on the seat, with the grain standing out a little, the pegs proud, and a general air of being used and worn and knocked about. Obvious places for wear and tear are the bottoms of the legs and the edges of the seat. Also, the underside of the overhang should show the patina of being picked up a million times by greasy fingers.

So, how do we fool our friends and neighbours? First, add wear, with glasspaper and a spokeshave or penknife. Don't overdo it, but allow no exposed line to be perfectly straight. Details of adding specific abuse are below; some is done before colouring, some after. There must also be general wear and tear, administered at random. Throw and drag your cut pieces of oak, and your completed stool before colouring, around the yard or along the street until you get a satisfactory number of chips and scratches. You can also hit it; a length of metal chain is excellent for a flogging.

Now, the colour. The best compromise between time and convenience is to steep your oak in cow muck. We realise this is not an option everyone can pursue, but then the best never is. The process gives you a very good colour which is not flat, as stain tends to be, but variegated in a natural, haphazard way.

You could go and collect a sack full of cow pats, make them into a soupy slop in a plastic dustbin, and immerse your stool in it. Add your used tea leaves and coffee grounds. You might be able to get hold of some horse manure instead or as well.

Much better, though, is to go down the village pub, make friends with a dairy farmer, buy him a pint and ask permission to use his slurry pit. He will think you insane, until you show him your finished antique. Slurry is a variable medium, its colouring powers being stronger or weaker depending on factors beyond your control. The specific gravity can vary also, so your oak may want to float. In any case, weigh it down with a good anchor, tie it securely to the land and mark the tie with something highly visible, so that an inattentive tractor driver doesn't go over it. Sorry, make that 'impossible to miss', not just highly visible (speaking from bitter personal experience). Remember also that a slurry pit is tidal. When you come to check it, the tide might be further in and your oak may be out of reach.

Four to six weeks will be a reasonable time in the pit but you don't want the colour to be too light. You can go to almost black for a very old and much used stool. A mid-term inspection will be necessary. Take some water with you, for example in a garden sprayer, to clean off the muck. The colour revealed when wet, is the colour you will get when it is polished.

Once you are satisfied with the colour, whether using dustbin method or slurry pit, you will have to get rid of the smell. A week in running water will do it, so it's handy to have your own trout stream or access thereto, or a week in the sea. Otherwise it's a fortnight or more in a water butt with regular water

This is a new oak joint stool, rather than a board stool, at the first stage of the ageing process: immersion in cow muck. This slurry, Holstein Fresian with some Jersey, is of slightly higher specific gravity than normal, possibly due to plentiful summer grass, so the unidentified shed-person is forced into submersive action.

Fortuitous crack and risen grain from soaking, peg standing proud, wear on the corner, random scratches and marks.

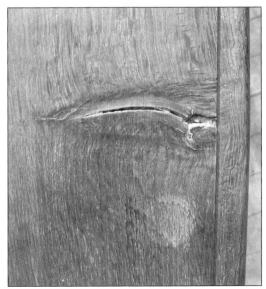

More damage from soaking, wear from a thousand hands and a mysterious circular mark.

changes, or lots of wet weather, or the equivalent in hosepipe soakings, or some of all of those. When the wood is wet, is the time to add wear to the bottoms of the leg pieces. Tap with a hammer to splay the feet and round them off, to simulate years of scraping on a stone floor.

Drying out in sun and wind between soakings seems to help lose the smell. Do not be dismayed by the light grey it goes when dry. Polish will bring all the colour back.

On no account use any household chemicals or proprietary deodorisers. These may spoil your colour and/or seal in the smell so it will never go.

Another great thing about soaking is that you are likely to get the odd random crack or two, which adds an authenticity you could never manufacture on purpose. It also raises the grain as if a hundred family backsides have gradually worn away the softer parts of the wood, leaving the harder grain standing out in tiny, well-polished ridges.

If cow muck is not for you, you have alternatives, such as burying in a peat bog for a year, or in your back garden for two, or making an acidic soil/compost-based sloppy mud in your dustbin. This will take longer than slurry – months rather than weeks.

Stain is the last resort because it tends to give a flat result and is the hardest to get right. If you have no other option but stain, then at least do a week or two's soaking in water, bash the feet, and allow the stool to dry out thoroughly, preferably in the sun. Mix dark oak stain with French polish, about 50:50. They don't blend, which is the idea. Try with a rag on a small area of the underside of the seat, or the inside of a leg. When dry, rub a little wax furniture polish on it. Does it look good?

Try more or less stain in the mix. When you like the result, slap it all over the stool with a brush. Do this at speed, with confidence. Don't worry about runs and uneven areas. Phew. Let's hope it works.

The fate of most of your stool's rustic and very early brethren was to be chopped up and put on the fire when the more elegant stuff came in. For it still to be here in the twenty-first century, it must have escaped from a number of small and very small accidents. It may have been through periods of indignity when, cast aside in favour of something new and fashionable, it was forgotten in the attic or left in the shed, or used for a lowlier purpose than that intended by the man who made it.

Antique dealers and knockers will pant inwardly with excitement at a good piece in a barn corner, unconsidered by its owner and abused for decades. It is only reasonable that your new antique should have suffered in the same way, to be rescued from that barn corner at last by your good self or other saintly person you know.

We give here a menu of possibilities for mistreatment, but be circumspect. No one piece could have suffered all of these miniature disasters. Beware of over faking.

Things to do before the colouring processes:

Story: It looks as if somebody's used it as a workbench.

Actuality: Whoever it was, he only used it as a workbench a few times. Put a piece of waste wood on your stool and saw through it, accidentally going too far. Repeat. Do the same with a drill and some different bit sizes.

Story: It looks like some kids have used it as a dartboard.

Actuality: Airgun pellets make good holes too.

Story: They must have had a dog that didn't like it. Look at the scratches.

Actuality: A dinner fork is good for making dog scratches. Use a dessert fork for cat scratches.

Story: Looks like something's bitten it.

Actuality: It was either a puppy having a chew, or you with a pair of pliers.

Story: We got the old paint off with stripper, which wasn't too difficult because somebody had done the worst of the job already, you know, all those layers of lead-based paint. If you look closely, you can see the marks of the blow lamp.

Actuality: Use a blow lamp to make a few burn marks, then sand them back a little.

Story: I wonder who AM was?

Actuality: Those old joiners often carved their initials on their work. On a stool, that would usually be on the top in a corner, or at the top of a leg. Practise your Roman lettering first; they were very good at it.

Story: I wonder whose shield it was?

Actuality: Rather than make a rudimentary coat of arms in negative as a branding iron, to burn the underside when making an inventory of household contents, you could draw it with a soldering iron.

After colouring, if some of your distressing has become too subtle, do it again, but you will probably reveal new wood beneath. Black shoe polish will sort that.

Now you can do the proper polishing. If using any method other than stain, once you are sure any smell has gone, rub all over with diluted French polish to seal and bring out the colour. Then, for all methods, wax polish except for the main underside, which never saw the light and was never touched. Use the finest grades of glasspaper to smooth those parts of the underside touched by fingers when lifting the stool, then double and treble polish.

Things to do after polishing:

Story: You can see where somebody has mended it, and not very well.
Actuality: Knock off a vulnerable bit and glue it back on. Use a visible glue such as Araldite.
Story: Somebody has obviously left it too near the fire.
Actuality: Use a blow lamp. Part of a stool could get badly scorched while the rest was untouched.
Story: Some careless party guest…
Actuality: Champagne is no good for decanter, bottle or wine-glass rings. You need something thick, red and sticky. Sloe gin is excellent, or elderberry wine. Also, maybe a cigar or cigarette fell out of the ashtray years ago, or a pen out of an inkwell.

You may well think of a few of your own accidents, and stories to tell the neighbours. Otherwise, that's it. Best of luck. Go on, you can do it.

TRUE OR FALSE?

How to make a Bigger Bang

If Guy Fawkes were around now, he would have a shed, no doubt about it. Should you wish to risk death or maiming in making the wherewithal for your own gunpowder plot, you can do so in your own shed with a few easily obtained ingredients. Should you succeed, there remains the distinct possibility of thereafter being hanged, drawn and quartered.

You make gun cotton by treating cotton with nitric acid, cotton being a nearly pure from of cellulose.

You cannot use gun-cotton directly in guns, as it is too violent and would blow them to pieces, but you can make a milder explosive by dissolving gun-cotton in acetone. The solution is dried and cut into cords, and is then known as cordite. Nitro-glycerine is a liquid explosive, which you can make by treating glycerine, a by-product of the soap industry, with nitric acid.

As you cannot conveniently use the liquid explosive, you soak it in an earthy powder. When this has set, you have the product known as dynamite.

The Noah's Ark of Sheds

'Make thee an ark of gopher wood; rooms shalt thou make in the ark, and shalt pitch it within and without with pitch'.

Genesis VI xiv

Dan McGrath may not have been expecting the end of the world, nor even a small earthquake or an inch or two of rain, but he surely was not going to have one of those sheds you can buy. He thought they were flimsy and expensive and would probably wobble in the wind. His shed was not going to wobble.

Subsidiary functional design criteria included wide doors, in case he wanted to put anything big in it and high doors so he didn't have to duck to come

A very secure and stable shed.

and go. Design preferences were for a square shed with a pavillion-style roof ('because they look cool and flat roofs are boring and leaky').

Enquiries at the wood merchant's regarding gopher wood produced less than satisfactory results, which is not surprising since no-one knows for certain what it is, or was, and so non-wobbliness began with integral four-inch corner posts sunk two feet into the ground and concreted in. This, says Dan, makes for a very secure and stable shed, and nobody would disagree with him on that.

The studwork of four-by-two timber, as can be seen from the picture, is similarly robust, while the floor joists are raised above the ground for dryness. Dan poured gravel into the gap between floor and earth 'to add extra strength', then fitted OSB on top (Oriented Strand Board it stands for, so please note that, like 'PIN number', 'OSB board' is a tautology).

Four triangles of OSB make a pointy pavillion roof. Calculating the triangle sizes was fairly complicated and calculating the angle of the edge cuts was even more so. Dan checked his figures with a cardboard scale model (presumably strong, thick cardboard), and decided on felt shingles to finish, rather than plain felt.

All roof joints and long expanses were reinforced with extra timber. The walls were to be of feather-edge boards but Dan had concerns about their

Little Emily in shed heaven.

ability to withstand weather, not to mention their contribution to overall sturdiness, so he clad the whole shed in sheets of 3mm plywood first, giving him the bonus of a nice finish inside. Rather than pitching within and without, Dan used wood preservatives unobtainable in Noah's time. After days and nights worrying about the wording, wife Sairee made a sign saying 'Dan's Shed', and that was that.

So happy with his shed was Dan that he built a garage in the same fashion (see picture with dartboard and spraying Emily), but used slightly less Armageddon-proof methods for his daughter's shed.

TRUE OR FALSE?

How Long for a Ptarmigan?

Many sheds are underused in the winter, which is the ideal season for hanging game. For those shed owners who wish to take advantage of this opportunity but are uncertain about the length of time needed for different species, here is a guide. We are assuming cold weather and an unheated shed, and that the animals are fresh when you get them.

Pheasants need ten days; partridge six to eight days; wild duck, seven; pigeons, four. All these should be hung undrawn. Grouse and ptarmigan, likewise undrawn, need three days, while quail, woodcock and snipe require only two.

Hares should be paunched and washed inside before hanging for six days. Treat a deer in the same way but hang for a fortnight.

Kostas Bozikis's shed again. From the outside it looks normal. He says: I am using my shed as a place where I can search for strange or curious things. I never remember where is what. So, it is like a treasure hunt. I am collecting everything under the sun. Basically Meccano and electronic parts. And I am lucky that the door of my shed opens outwards, otherwise I couldn't open it.

Where the Jazz Lamp Shines Brightly

When the word 'jazz' isn't being used musically, it can be used to describe fantastical designs and vivid patterns, and the Jersey Lily (Langtry) was a fairly flamboyant character, which probably explains how one of Pauline Holt's daughters came to rename her mother Jazzy Lily.

This particular Lily has spent a great part of her life learning about jewellery, starting as a girl assistant in a Manchester shop, moving on to a diploma in gemology and membership of the National Association of Goldsmiths. There was no thought at that stage of membership of another great body, the tribe of the Sheddici, because her moment didn't come until October 1997 when she happened to look around a bead fair in Ealing. There she was transfixed by a brilliant display of vibrantly coloured glass put on by the firm of Plowden

Come on, babe. Why don't we paint the town? And all that jazz.

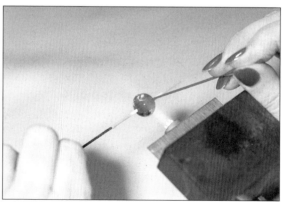

Each bead is individually lamp worked. The end of a glass rod is heated to a molten state then wrapped around a steel mandrel. By rotating the mandrel while continuing to heat the glass, the forces of surface tension and gravity allow a bead to form. By applying small amounts of different coloured molten glass to the bead while it's still hot, the maker creates patterns and decorations which fuse into the bead. Thus each bead is unique and a work of art in its own right, in the shed.

Interesting, but it's not a brewery

One excellent use for a shed is as a House of Fermentation, and there are many proprietary and inspirational routes to SPA (Shed Pale Ale) and Shedneuf du Pape. Here we offer fermented liquor made chiefly from an ingredient found growing freely near many sheds: nettles.

The original Sheddici would not have used hops in their beer but may have added flavour and preservative qualities with other herbs, such as ground ivy, *Glechoma hederacea*, and there's no reason why you cannot use it too, if you can be bothered to pick it. Meanwhile, put on a pair of stout gloves and gather about a pound or half a kilo of young nettle tops, plus a handful of whatever herbs you might have growing, for example rosemary, sage, thyme, lemon balm and loveage, but probably not chives.

Put your collected greenery in a large pan, add the grated rind of a lemon, and pour on boiling water to cover. Give a good stir, put the pan on the stove to bring the aromatic silage back to the boil, let it stand for a quarter of an hour to mash, and strain into another vessel. You are looking for half a gallon of liquid (two and a half litres if you're using metric quantities), so add water to make up as necessary and the juice of the lemon in any case.

Dissolve half a pound (250g) of Demerara sugar and half an ounce (15g) of cream of tartar in your liquor. When the whole business is down to lukewarm, add some brewer's yeast according to the instructions on the packet. Experienced home-brewers will know what to do next. Inexperienced ones must be informed that the vinegar fly is the enemy, and so your brew must be tightly covered or protected by an air-lock, so that carbon dioxide can bubble out but the dreaded little mite can't get in.

When it has stopped bubbling, decant into supremely clean bottles – plastic soft-drink bottles are good, also screw-top wine bottles – into each of which you have placed a half teaspoon or so of sugar per pint. It should be refizzed and ready in a week.

If you think this sound like a lot of bother for four pints of nettle beer, remember it's costing you almost nothing. You can scale the recipe up, but you might like to try it first.

& Thompson of Stourbridge, who describe themselves as a long-established glass manufacturer for industrial, medical, commercial and recreational uses, serving customers with a range of coloured rod, powders, chips, tube and raw materials.

P & T also run courses in glass bead-making. Lily enrolled. She bought a book about making glass beads, took it home and read it from cover to cover, marvelling at the beautiful photographs. She went on more courses in America, where bead-making is big.

You use a propane and oxygen torch which gives out a long, extremely hot flame and a lot of noise. It's called lampworking. You need all the aforementioned rods, powders and so on, and you need a place to do it in. Here came the shed but, being Jazzy Lily, it couldn't stay as bought. It had to be decorated inside and out to look like a Caribbean beach hut.

Lily now wishes she'd got a larger one but, with careful organisation, she has found room for all her glass, enamel powders, silver leaf and tools, plus a small kiln for annealing, which toughens and makes more permanent the designs on the finished article. The heat from torch and kiln make a stove in the shed unnecessary.

Jazzy Lily founded Glass Beadmakers UK (www.gbuk.org), the only society of its kind in Britain and, would you believe it, of course you would, she now teaches bead-making on her own courses at Plowden & Thompson. See www.jazzylily.com.

The Mothers of Invention

A s many famous inventors have shown, the shed is the ideal place for thinking revolutionary thoughts and for building prototypes without having anyone there to laugh at you. Whether it's a purpose-built workshop, a general shed or an old lean-to, there is something about a shed that promotes creative ideas. Not all of them come to anything, sometimes because of the lack of imagination in potential investors, sometimes because the invention is rubbish, but that doesn't mean we should stop trying. Take, for example, the case of Mr Frank Wainwright, surveyor, of Edgware, Middlesex.

Wainwright's Improved Closet Seat (patent number 24194/1901) recognised that it is frequently desirable that in a closet for general use there should be provided a separate seat for the principal or for members of the family.

Mr Wainwright, pondering in his shed, came up with a two-seat answer to this perennial problem. The lower seat was for general use, while a special upper one could fold down over it. To avoid the embarrassment of the wrong bottom on the wrong seat, the upper one would be locked upright, the key being in the possession of the person or persons having the entitlement to use it.

Eugene Graves and William Brown of Black River, New York, USA, were gentlemen of independent means and so had no need of financial reward. It was the spirit of invention that drove them. When Brown came to call, Mrs Graves would direct him to the shed down the garden where, almost certainly, he would find his friend busy with some invention or other.

One day, Graves was fiddling around with a table-top version of Aunt Sally. He had rigged up a small, fixed catapult and was firing dried beans from it, at a row of wine corks a few feet away.

'What ho,' said Brown. 'A new game?'

'Well, sort of,' said Graves, 'but I think I'm missing something.'

'Tell you what,' said Brown. 'Build a miniature gibbet, and dangle some miniature miscreants from it, and have them standing on the corks. So, when you knock a cork out with a bean from the catapult, the model criminal takes the fatal drop.'

'Brilliant,' said Graves. 'And we'll use marbles instead of beans.'

Thus was born Graves and Brown's Improved Game (US patent 1860/1902). We think the patent must have run out by now, and so the way is open for anyone to improve the game even further. It needn't be a catapult, for instance.

Walter Winans, another American but one residing near Ashford, Kent, was troubled by the likelihood of getting lost while out shooting in a wild region. Given to trumpet practice in his shed, where nobody could hear him, he had the idea of modifying the trumpet mouthpiece so it would fit into the barrel of a shotgun, at the stock end where the cartridge would normally go. The barrel would thus be transformed into a herald's coach horn, providing the means whereby other shooters in the party could be alerted to the blower's distress. Winans's Improved Alarm Call for Sportsmen was patented in 1904, number 2266.

When home from the sea, the Lincolnshire sailor Thomas Anderson liked to try out in his shed the various ideas that had occurred to him while crossing the trackless ocean. One such was his Device for Holding Down Ladies' Dress Skirts (patent number 14788) when the wearer was cycling, walking, playing tennis or taking other exercise. A metal bracelet fitted around one of the lady's ankles, with rods radiating from it that could be attached to the inside lining of the skirt, thus keeping the hem firmly in line.

Realising that it needed some sort of emergency release mechanism, he made an arrangement of springs that would work automatically if, as he put it, the skirt 'was subjected to excessive strain'.

Alas, he underestimated the fashionable variations in Edwardian skirt sizes and, after a series of unfortunate accidents, had to withdraw his device from sale.

Edible gramophone records, a device for informing passers-by in the cemetery that a person had been buried alive, a machine for projecting elephants into the air so they can do somersaults, a double-bladed breadknife to cut two slices at once – these and many more sparkling ideas have occurred to occupiers of sheds, which is proof, if proof were needed, of the intellect-comforting atmosphere that pervades our favourite haunt.

Shed Prevents that Sinking Feeling

Chris Anderson lives near the rivers Derwent and Ouse, in the East Riding not far from Selby, and he fancied having a boat. He also fancied the idea of a restoration, so when he had a chance to get hold of an old pleasure cruiser in dire need of repair, he took it without hesitation.

The first priority was to see what he'd let himself in for, which meant a forensic examination, starting with stripping the paint on the hull back to bare wood. Imagine his surprise when he found the name *Losada, Liverpool* branded into the back of the boat. The *Losada*, he discovered, had been a merchant ship of the Pacific Steam Navigation Company, a firm started in 1838 in London by one William Wheelwright, who was well connected in Chile and those kinds of places, and this wreck of a pleasure cruiser had been one of the *Losada's* lifeboats.

No, no, it's not Noah. He's on page 127.

Chris completely renovated the hull, replacing planks as necessary, re-painted and launched her into the Derwent with the hull fully finished. The idea was to complete the superstructure and fit out the interior of the cabin with *Wayfarer*, as she was now known, at a mooring, because the fees for hardstanding were over budget.

With the sun not quite over the yard-arm one summer's afternoon, person or persons unknown, very probably of the Just William variety, set the *Wayfarer* adrift. She floated downstream and got stuck under the Loftsome Bridge. Nothing could be done until the waters receded somewhat, which they did, when a routine opening of the tidal barrage at Barmby (to let water into the Ouse) left the *Wayfarer* sitting on pilings that pierced her bottom. She fell over sideways and sank.

A rescue mission was successfully mounted and the *Wayfarer* returned to the boatyard, there to await a resurgence of inspiration from her owner. A resurgence of funds would have been good too, but with the needs of a young family coming first, the *Wayfarer* never got far up the list of priorities.

Chris brought her back home and put her in the garden, hoping that enthusiasm would ensue but it never did, even though parting with her was not an option to be contemplated. Eventually Karen, wife thereof, suggested making a part of the *Wayfarer* into a shed. Brilliant.

The bows were separated from the rest, and fittings salvaged. There she stands, complete with brass wossname rope-windy things as door handles, and port and starboard navigation lights that now act as candle holders, glowing red and green as per. Once again for those readers looking in black

MV Losada, *here pictured coming in to Liverpool, her home port, in 1951, is not on fire but rather awaiting the attentions of an invisible smoky old tug. A lifeboat, possibly the very lifeboat in question, can just be seen slung over the side in front of the rear mast.*

and white, the green light is on the right and so assumes that the ship/shed is sailing upwards to the sky.

Losada was built in 1921 by Harland & Wolff, Glasgow, 6,520 tons gross, 4,021 net, 406 feet long. She would have been on the west coast South America run, taking mail in both directions plus general cargo outbound, possibly including livestock, and homeward bound probably copper, cotton, fishmeal, onions and melons depending upon the season. She was broken up in 1952.

Capital of the Welsh Empire

Uncle Wilco (real name Roger Wilco), Emperor of Sheds, guides his subjects with a gentle hand from a secret valley in a place best known in the newspapers as a unit of measurement (3,000,000 football pitches = 1 Wales; 3 Waleses = 2 Belgiums).

Way back in the year 2000, as the third millennium dawned over a hopeful world, Uncle Wilco decided that a new shed would be the ideal metaphorical vehicle in which to move forward into the twenty-first century. Searching the relatively undeveloped internet of the time, he was confounded to see that there was no website devoted to sheds. In his ears rang the words that A.E. Housman almost wrote: 'If a man will comprehend the richness and variety of the universe, and inspire his mind with a due measure of wonder and awe, he must contemplate the shed not only on its heights of genius but in its abysses of ineptitude'.

So, Wilco had a mission: to offer an ethereal platform for sheds in all their infinite miscellany.

The matter was discussed with like-minded fellows in several places of refreshment, and Wilco went home to register the domain name. Unfortunately, due to over enthusiasm, he made a slight error. The choice of name had been based on the title of a well-known if scurrilous publication featuring photographs of the wives of literate men, but it came out as 'readersheds', which nobody can understand.

The work involved in setting up a large website must not be underestimated. At times, Uncle Wilco felt himself flagging but was always reinvigorated by the support of the shed community. He also claims to have gathered new inspiration from a previous publication by this correspondent and owns four copies of it. Some responsibility for his obsession must therefore be admitted, but not much.

He describes his own shed as humble and green, with a leak in the roof and a comfortable chair. In this chair he can gaze emotionally at a signed photograph of the television personality Sarah Beeny, she of *The Property Ladder* on Channel 4 and, more famously, judge of The Shed of the Year competition on Wilco's website. The Uncle/Emperor can also watch the spiders who call his shed home, raise a glass of Bull's Blood to Sarah, and occasionally indulge in normal shed activities such as trying to raise plants from seed.

Meanwhile, seedlings forgotten and neglected on their shelves, his brain whirrs constantly as he plans the future of his ever-expanding realm, including the removal of the computerised tools of government from the marital bricks and mortar to permit the installation thereof in the shed. Already he has electricity.

See the Shed of the Year competition. Read the Shed Blog. Go to readersheds. co.uk.

The Joke Shed

No matter what your mood, you really can't help but warm to St Helens comedian Dave Twentyman. His cheeky, chatty style endears him to the toughest of audiences. It's light-hearted, positive fun, keeping the laughter flowing.

Had you occasion to visit any of such select venues as Jongleurs, Liverpool Rawhide, The Last Laugh – Sheffield, The Hyena – Newcastle, Just The Tonic – Nottingham, and many more in London, Edinburgh and all over the place, you would not need to be told this by Dave's PR. What you might not know is that he recharges his comic muse in his shed.

He set himself up with telly, Playstation, stove and comfy chair. It is his getaway, his relaxing space, not overlooked, not in anyone's road. Wife Susan never bothers him, except to send a text asking if he wants a cup of tea.

Knock, knock. Who's there? Susan. Susan who? Susan your dinner's in the dog.

The children, Olivia aged four and Matthew, two, are not allowed access ('they might mess it up') but, as anyone who ever had a young family will agree, space in the house can become scarcer and scarcer. Dave feels himself gradually being hijacked. He is, by nature, an easy-going fellow, so Susan – looking for somewhere to put something, such as a fire surround or a rug – will always say to herself 'Oh, he won't mind'.

'I have to climb over stuff just to get in,' says the peeved comedian. 'Every bit of space I get, she takes it.'

Come on, Dave, we know you don't mean that. Get a bigger shed. Meanwhile, here is a special joke, written by Dave Twentyman exclusively for the readers of this book. Thus:

It was well after closing time. Everybody had finished their drinks and left, except for one morose-looking chap. 'Ain't you got no 'ome to go to?' said the landlady, gently but firmly.

'That's the trouble,' said the man. 'My wife's been and thrown me out. She says it won't make any difference to her. I spend all my time in my shed anyway. So she's put a padlock on it and bolted our front door.'

'One more pint, but you'll have to go by half past,' said the landlady.

'I really miss her now I haven't got her. She's always looked after me. Been there for me, you know, no matter what. A friend in need. You don't realise what you've got until it's too late.'

'It's never too late,' said the landlady. 'Ring her. Tell her what you just told me.'

'Ring who?'

'Ring your wife.'

'I'm not talking about my wife. I'm talking about my shed.'

Just an Old-Fashioned Shed

There are many remarkable sheds and sheddists in this book, so perhaps we should finish with a word about the shed of olden days, the shed that granddad had. It was his territory; the place trouble could not invade. It was the store where he kept those special things, the value of which could not be understood by grandma. If she ever went in the shed, she would shake her head with a tut-tut, and say 'I don't know what you want this old rubbish for'.

The mysterious Miss X and her heart's desire.

Although there were many eccentric and individualistic members of the Sheddici around then – George Bernard Shaw, for example, famously wrote in his shed – granddad's shed was almost certainly to do with gardening.

It was the type of shed that didn't attract attention; it did not invite visitors. It may even have been partly hidden from view, reached only by a secret path of broken bricks that meandered between bushes, or had about it a look of abandonment.

But forget granddad and grandma. If we want a shed of today, at the other end of the scale from the starlit palaces seen elsewhere in these pages, we need look no further than the British standard allotment. Miss X and her allotment shed fill the bill very nicely, certainly having that look of abandonment (the

shed, not Miss X), with space only sufficient to fit in the basic gardening tools, a few odds and ends, and either the ancient rotavator or Miss X, but not both at the same time.

For reasons we are about to explain, we cannot reveal the location of Miss X's shed, nor her name. She is a Mistress of Disguise and has been photographed wearing a wig. Although here representing something typical, she herself is anything but.

She may be a recent convert to shedding, and to vegetable growing, and she may not yet know her Hurst Greenshaft from her Imperial Longpod, or her Lingua di Fucco from her Amsterdam Forcing, but she will, dear reader, she will.

Rumours abound in the village pub where she is occasionally glimpsed. There are stories of Hollywood. We do know that Miss X went to drama school, so perhaps there is a grain of truth in that one about the MGM executive who tried to lure Miss X on to the casting couch and ended up in an ambulance.

The other story is that she was an undercover farmer's wife, mucking out the pigs in rural obscurity and churning out three Sunday dinners a day, rather than be kidnapped by agents of the Sultan of somewhere who wanted her for his senior concubine.

But we must stop there. We are doing her no favours. Miss X simply wants to grow her butternut squashes, her leeks and her marigolds, away from the public gaze, the red carpet and the glare of flash photography, and now and then shelter from the rain in an old-fashioned shed by an old-fashioned fence, with an old-fashioned fellow to start the rotavator for her.

It's Kostas, thinking of strange and curious things.

And these are the things of which he is thinking.